London 1952
Buses, Trams & Trolleybuses

Philip Wallis

Ian Allan
PUBLISHING

Above: The forecourts of London pubs were often used as termini for bus routes. This practice dated back to horse-bus days, when the draught animals bringing the buses would be offered fodder and water at such termini — with refreshment for the crews clearly available too! The practice continued into motor-bus days and was not confined to 'occasional use only' either, as evidenced by this 1952 gathering of seven RTs and one 10T10 lined up along the forecourt of the Royal Forest Hotel at Chingford. Routes terminating here were the trunk 38 to Victoria, 102 to Golders Green and 145 to Dagenham, and single-deck route 205 to Hammond Street; the intensity of services was such that LT even provided a mobile staff canteen at this location. *C. Carter*

Front cover:

Tramcar No 82 has just arrived at Middle Park Avenue, Eltham Green, terminus of route 44 in June 1952. The conductor heads back to the platform, having just lowered the forward trolley pole whilst his motorman raises the rear trolley pole onto the outer overhead wire, after which he will drive the tramcar forward over a crossover before heading back to Woolwich. Part of London Transport's elderly tram fleet, tramcar 82 was an 'E/1' class dating from 1927 and was operated originally by East Ham Corporation. The advertisements carried symbolised the transition that London Transport was going through

in 1952: the enamelled, permanently-fixed plate promoting 'Oakey's Genuine Emery Cloth' evokes memories of the tramways' prewar heyday; the Hovis display, making bold use of lower-case lettering, symbolises expectations of modernity at the dawn of the New Elizabethan Age. *C. Carter*

Back cover (upper):

London Transport's attention to detail is emphasised by two inspectors supervising departures of tram-replacement bus routes on a frosty weekday in January 1952 at Baring Road bus stand, Grove Park. RTs 2733, 2754 and 3391 were amongst those buses allocated to the new Rye Lane garage, which first became operational on 6 January 1952 following Stage 6 of Operation Tramway. Bus routes 149 and 179 replaced tram routes 52 and 74 respectively, whilst bus route 69, on which the driver of RT3391 sits in the cab turning the final destination indicator waiting for 'VICTORIA' to appear, replaced tram route 54. *C. F. Klapper / The Omnibus Society*

Back cover (lower):

This section of Holloway Road at the 'Nag's Head', seen in March 1952, was served principally by electrically-powered road passenger transport, this comprising eight trolleybus routes and one tram route. Conduit-powered 'E/3'-class tram No 1980 is bound for Forest Hill, 1¼ hours' travelling time distant on Kingsway Subway route 35. 'J3'-class trolleybus No 1033 will continue its long uphill run along the A1 road to North Finchley, while 'K'-class trolleybus No 1101 on route 679 will parallel the tram route as far as St John Street, Islington. *C. Carter*

First published 2001

ISBN 0 7110 2806 0

All rights reserved. No part of this book may be reproduced or transmitted in any form or by any means, electronic or mechanical, including photocopying, recording or by any information storage and retrieval system, without permission from the Publisher in writing.

© Ian Allan Publishing Ltd 2001

Published by Ian Allan Publishing

an imprint of Ian Allan Publishing Ltd, Hersham, Surrey KT12 4RG. Printed by Ian Allan Printing Ltd, Hersham, Surrey KT12 4RG.

Code: 0109/B1

Contents

Author's Note

This book is substantially based on the records and reminiscences of Richard Forall. In 1952 Richard, aged in his early 20s, lived with his parents at Reading. Following National Service in the Army he was employed by local bus company, Thames Valley, as a management trainee. Membership of the Southern Counties Touring Society had led to his forming a friendship with John Ryder who, having completed National Service with the Royal Air Force, was a student at Reading University. Both young men's interest in transport prompted them to sample as much as they could of London Transport's varied operations in 1952. London was relatively accessible from Reading, both by rail to Paddington and by Thames Valley limited-stop bus routes A and B, which terminated at Victoria Coach Station.

Where detail in Richard Forall's notes was incomplete, contemporary or other authoritative sources have been consulted. The opening and final chapters of the book have been added to expand more fully upon the scale, structure and variety of London Transport's bus, tram and trolleybus operations. Otherwise, the book is an account of travel by both vintage and modern buses, tramcars and trolleybuses around London Transport's area in 1952.

Philip Wallis
Bramley, Hampshire
May 2001

Above: No fewer than 531 new RT-family double-deckers were delivered to London Transport in 1952 — an average of 10 per week. Brand-new Weymann-bodied AEC Regent 3RT RT3545 (MLL 855), allocated to Catford garage, is seen on Last Tram Day (5 July 1952) coping with Saturday-afternoon crowds in Woolwich. Lack of a front route-number blind has led to the improvised use of a side display blind in the intermediate destination box. *W.J.Wyse, courtesy G.W.Morant*

Below: High-frequency route 227 was the third Central Area bus route to receive new RF-class saloons which displaced venerable LT 'Scooters'. Metro-Cammell-bodied AEC Regal IV RF331 (MLL 968), a 41-seater allocated to Bromley garage, is seen in Bromley Market Place on its first Saturday in service, 8 November 1952. *G.W.Morant*

1

The Executive

1952 — the most momentous peacetime year for London Transport since its formation in 1933. The keynote of the year was modernisation, resulting in a sea-change in the types of vehicles providing London's road passenger transport, such that by the year end almost 80% of scheduled mileage was worked by postwar RT-family double-deckers and RF coaches and saloons. The last trams, which mode of transport had been a cornerstone of London's road passenger transport since the beginning of the century, with origins dating back to 1861, were withdrawn. That other form of electrically-propelled street transport in the Metropolis, the trolley-bus system, took delivery of 50 new trolleybuses fated to be the system's last new vehicles. By contrast, 902 new diesel-engined buses and coaches joined the fleet,

giving an average intake of 75 vehicles per month. The main problem faced by London Transport's management was that of maintaining a proper balance between revenue and expenditure. Despite a fall of 4.4% in the number of journeys originating on the London Transport system (including Underground railways), to 4,295 million, an alarming deficit on road passenger services of over £2 million the previous year in net traffic receipts, the difference between fares collected and operating expenses was reduced to £300,000 in 1952. Encouraging growth trends were evident in the Country Bus & Coach Department, boosted by growing populations at six New Towns within its area — Crawley, Harlow, Hatfield, Hemel Hempstead, Stevenage and Welwyn — as well as at 'out-country' London County Council housing estates and other developments, and

Below: 'E/3'-class tramcars Nos 1926 and 1996, seen outside New Cross depot on Last Tram Day — 5 July 1952. While this scene induces nostalgia for enthusiasts, it also shows why London's trams were regarded as a danger and inconvenience to other road users. Inspector and passengers take their chances with oncoming traffic, including an RT on tram-replacement bus route 69 (Grove Park–Victoria), to gain access to their tram. Both cars are on short workings to New Cross Gate and will cause further traffic disruption as they execute crossover manœuvres. *W. J. Wyse, courtesy G. W. Morant*

Above: In pristine condition, 70-seat Metro-Cammell-bodied BUT 9641T 'Q1'-class trolleybus No 1862 (LYH 862), allocated to Isleworth, passes along Chiswick High Road *en route* from Shepherd's Bush to Hounslow, shortly after entering service. *R. H. G. Simpson*

Right: London Transport's wartime utility buses which, apart from the Daimlers, had never been popular with crews and the trade union, faced the axe by 1952. No G66 (GLL 566), a Park Royal-bodied Guy Arab I of 1943, had been relegated to training duties at Alperton garage by the time this view was taken in 1952. *Aviation & Transport Photographs, courtesy R. Marshall*

Below: Immediate postwar LT policy, which concentrated investment in new double-deck buses, led to an increasingly-elderly single-deck fleet; the advent of the RF class in 1951 heralded the beginning of a rapid update. This took time to complete, and many veterans, such as three-axle LGOC-bodied AEC Renown LT1015 (GO 648), continued in service during 1952. The Bell Punch-equipped conductor enjoys the sunshine whilst his bus lays over in Cromwell Road, Kingston, before proceeding to the bus station to take up a journey on route 213 to Sutton garage, where it was based. *V. C. Jones / Ian Allan Library*

further helped by the absorption of the former Eastern National local services in the Grays area; passenger loadings showed a healthy 2.4% increase. Passengers using Green Line coaches clearly appreciated the completion in 1952 of a rapid modernisation programme of the network's fleet to include 232 RF-class coaches, yielding the network a very impressive 11.3% increase in passenger journeys. London Transport was investing heavily in improved premises too. During 1952 four brand-new bus garages were opened, whilst a further two former tramway premises were converted for use by buses. Work was also underway on extending and equipping Aldenham Works for its future destiny as the repair and overall centre for London Transport's bus and coach fleet.

Organisation

London Transport was by far the country's largest road passenger transport operator, serving an area of 2,000 square miles with a population of 9.8 million. At 1 January 1952 LT owned 8,477 diesel-engined buses and coaches, 1,773 trolleybuses and 378 tramcars (detailed in Appendices 1-3). Not all these vehicles were available for use, as the total stock included new vehicles received from manufacturers but not yet licensed,

GREEN LINE TRANSFORMATION

Right: Conversion of scheduled single-deck Green Line routes to RF operation was completed by 1 November 1952. A 39-seat Metro-Cammell-bodied AEC Regal IV, RF163 (MLL 550), is seen at the Eccleston Bridge (Victoria) mid-point of route 702 (Gravesend–Sunningdale) in July 1952. *G.H.F.Atkins*

Below: The Green Line fleet had always featured innovative vehicle designs, perhaps none more so than the side-engined AEC Q class. The 32-seat centre-entrance 6Q6 variant was introduced in 1936 especially for Green Line service, to which the type returned after wartime duty as ambulances. Q194 (CXX 387) is seen at Hertford bus station on 20min-frequency, 50-mile-long route 715 to Guildford, which completed conversion to RF class in January 1952. This coach was one of 20 6Q6s which from March 1952 saw a few additional months' service at Muswell Hill garage, where they were sent to replace single-deck LT-class AEC Renown saloons following repeated complaints from passengers and staff alike about the condition of the latter. *G.W.Morant*

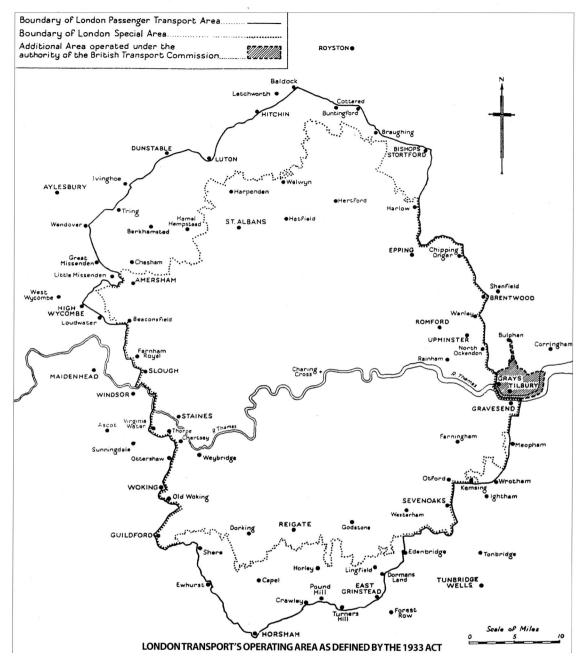

LONDON TRANSPORT'S OPERATING AREA AS DEFINED BY THE 1933 ACT

Within the London Special Area, LT enjoyed a monopoly of bus-service provision. Apart from being allowed to work in for up to ½ mile to reach a terminus, other operators had to obtain LT's 'consent' to work in this area. As LT's policy was to operate all ordinary bus services in the London Special Area itself, very few 'consents' were granted.

In the areas between the boundary of the London Special Area and the boundary of the London Passenger Transport Area, LT had to apply for Road Service Licences as could other operators. Bus services in these areas were provided either by LT or by independents, since the neighbouring 'provincial operating companies' — which included

Aldershot & District, Eastern National, Maidstone & District, Southdown and Thames Valley — were effectively barred from working there under the terms of the 1933 Act.

LT enjoyed limited running rights beyond the boundary of the LPTA to certain specified destinations. In reciprocation, limited running rights existed for other operators to reach certain specified destinations within the LPTA. On 30 September 1951 LT's operating area had been further extended by the addition of territory around Grays and Tilbury formerly worked by BTC-controlled Eastern National.

Norbiton was LT's fourth brand-new postwar bus garage to be opened, on 14 May 1952. With an initial allocation of 58 buses, it took the pressure off the overcrowded Kingston garage, which up until then had had to park 32 buses 'off premises' overnight. The new garage was also planned to incorporate maintenance facilities for other garages, being provided with nine maintenance pits and thus designed to handle up to 275 buses. Norbiton took over Kingston's allocation on routes 65, 131, 206, 213 and 264, as well as Turnham Green's share of the 65. Paradoxically, Norbiton, whose architectural style reflected the growing postwar confidence of both London Transport and the nation as a whole, inherited seven of LT's oldest buses — 1929 T-class AEC Regals — from Kingston for use on route 264. *London Transport*

delicensed stock held in reserve and withdrawn vehicles awaiting disposal. A more accurate guide to the scale of operations was evident from the number of vehicles scheduled for use on Monday-Friday peak-hour work — the busiest time of the week. On that same date 7,012 buses and coaches, 1,603 trolleybuses and 323 tramcars were allocated to duties. To operate these vehicles over 7,566 miles of service route, 47,000 drivers and conductors were employed, supervised by 2,500 inspectors. To keep the vehicles themselves on the road, a further 17,000 staff worked on servicing, overhaul, repair and cleaning duties at both Chiswick and Aldenham Works as well as at 88 bus garages and 23 tram or trolleybus depots (detailed in Appendices 4-7).

Further staff were employed in administrative, technical, clerical and control duties, whilst yet more worked in electrical engineering, in the Works & Building Department and on welfare duties. London Transport was a very large organisation indeed; including Underground railway staff, it employed 100,000 people in 1952.

Left: Typifying the fine body of men and women at the sharp end is this group of five drivers and Bell Punch-equipped conductors dressed in LT uniform, seen standing at the entrance to New Cross depot on 5 January 1952. Their smart appearance is indicative of the disciplined society that existed in 1952, at a time when 18-year-old males were liable to undertake National Service in the Armed Forces. The noticeboard behind the men is aimed at contractors undertaking work on converting New Cross from tram depot to bus garage. *G.W. Morant*

London Transport had been created by the London Passenger Transport Act (1933 Act, from here on), which came into effect on 1 July 1933. The Act united London General — until then London's biggest bus operator — and most other bus and all tramway and trolleybus interests in the London area, along with the Metropolitan and Underground railways, to form the London Passenger Transport Board. Following direct Government control under emergency powers enacted at the start of World War 2, ultimate responsibility for the renamed London Transport Executive had passed to the British Transport Commission (BTC) on 1 January 1948. The BTC had itself been created by the immediate postwar Labour Government, strongly committed to

nationalisation of the nation's key industries, including transport. The main-line railways, many docks and harbours, cross-channel ferries and much long-distance road haulage became BTC-controlled. Significant bus-operating interests sold out to the BTC from 1948 onwards, including former London operator Thomas Tilling Ltd, which by then controlled a substantial number of provincial bus operators.

The BTC was charged with providing (or ensuring the provision of) a co-ordinated and efficient system of public transport (except by air) and port facilities for passengers and goods throughout the country, with due regard to safety of operation. Day-to-day management was vested in various 'Executives', one of which was the

London Transport Executive, which still remained a statutory body under the 1933 Act, with its duties assigned to it in a rather formal manner. Because of this, appointments to the Executive were made directly by the Minister of Transport and not by the BTC. The result was a two-tier management structure, considered by some contemporary observers to blur financial imperatives at London Transport. The Executive, chaired by Lord Latham, comprised four other full-time and two part-time members. LT's headquarters were at 55 Broadway, Westminster.

Central Road Services

In October 1950 LT's formerly-separate Central Bus and Tram & Trolleybus operating departments had been merged together into a new Central Road Services organisation, which became responsible for all red-liveried London Transport vehicles operating broadly within the Metropolitan Police District. Central Road Services itself was divided into four more-or-less equally-sized Divisions: North West, North East, South East and South West. Each had a manager who was responsible for operations from all motor-bus garages and tram and trolleybus depots within his Division.

By 1952 LT was well into its commitment to replacing the tram system with diesel buses. All of London's tramways in East and West London — as well as most tram routes in North London — had been converted to trolleybus operation in a massive prewar conversion programme that was halted by hostilities in 1940. After the war, LT had announced its intention to continue with the tramway-abandonment programme, but with the important difference that diesel-engined buses (rather than trolleybuses) would replace the remaining

tramcars. On 5 July 1950 Lord Latham announced Operation Tramaway, with a plan to replace London's remaining trams with buses in nine stages between October 1950 and October 1952. By 1 January 1952 the first five stages of Operation Tramaway had been implemented, with tram routes in the Battersea, Croydon, Clapham, Dulwich, Streatham and Walworth areas replaced by motor-bus routes. In another important policy move, LT had in 1949 adopted a decision in principle to replace its trolleybus system with motor buses, with the expectation that replacement would start in the late 1950s when the bulk of the trolleybus fleet, dating from the 1930s, would be time-expired.

Trams

Despite the considerable depletion of the fleet from its prewar zenith (or even immediate postwar size of approximately 900 trams), at the beginning of 1952 LT's fleet of 378 tramcars still ranked as the fifth-largest tramway undertaking in the country, being exceeded in size only by the municipal fleets at Leeds (396), Sheffield (444), Liverpool (499) and Glasgow (1,173). In Appendix 4 it can be seen that LT's remaining trams operated from four depots, with a maximum of 332 cars scheduled for use on a Saturday.

London's tramway system was powered by conduit or overhead current collection. This came about because the former London County Council (LCC) tramway predominantly used the conduit system, which allowed a tram to pick up power from an under-ground conductor rail through the use of a 'plough'. The system avoided the use of overhead wires with supporting poles, which were likely to attract objections in some of the inner London areas where LCC trams operated. Outer-

Above left: Despite imminent closure of the network, essential maintenance work on London's tram tracks had to continue. In this scene on the Embankment just south of Hungerford Bridge, caught by the camera on 15 March 1952, workmen stand clear to allow the passage of northbound former Leyton Corporation 'E/3'-class tramcar No 176 before returning to their task. An RT on tram-replacement route 109 heads southwards using the same section of road as the tramway. *J. C. Gillham*

Above: The plough-shifter at Lee Green holds in his right hand a special fork in which rests a 'plough'; in his left he holds a tool which he will use to push the plough towards the tram along the curved conduit slot as he walks forward beside the slow-moving car. When the plough has gained a central position in a carrier underneath the tram, the fork will be withdrawn. A few yards further along, the driver will stop and operate a changeover switch from overhead to conduit power operation whilst his conductor will stow and secure the trolley pole. In a reverse procedure for changing from conduit to overhead power operation, the plough will be shot out from underneath a tram car along the conduit slot on the right-hand side. Two spare ploughs for subsequent use are lined up in the conduit slot. *J. C. Gillham*

Left: Despite the standardisation for which London Transport was renowned, some oval tram-stop signs of London County Council origin remained in use until closure of the tramway system. This request stop was photographed on 29 June 1952 in Camberwell New Road — by then served by tram routes 40 and 72 only. In accordance with LT practice, the stop used by parallel bus routes was sited a short distance beyond the tram stop. *J. C. Gillham*

Above: Route 607 (Shepherd's Bush–Uxbridge) had a journey time of one hour, and maintaining a frequency of up to two minutes required 75 trolleybuses — the highest allocation for any individual trolleybus route in 1952. All-Leyland 'F1' class No 722 (DLY 722) of 1937, seen in Hanwell Broadway, was allocated to Hanwell depot. *A. D. Packer, courtesy J. C. Gillham.*

suburban tram routes had been developed both by company operators and by several municipalities which had opted for cheaper-to-install overhead-wire current-collection systems, with tramcars using a trolley pole to collect current from the wire. With increased route co-ordination the use of both methods of power collection became common on different sections of the same route, necessitating the provision of a London tramway institution — the 'change-pit' — at all points where the method of power supply changed. Five change-pits still existed along routes at the beginning of 1952.

A Central Repair Department at Charlton, in South East London, was responsible for tram overhaul and maintenance. As most redundant London trams would be scrapped, a breaker's yard in Penhall Road, near Charlton Works, was commissioned in 1950. Dubbed the 'Tramatorium', Penhall Road could hold about 150 cars on 34 tracks connected by a traverser.

Trolleybuses

London Transport's fleet of 1,773 trolleybuses dwarfed in scale the operations of even the nation's largest municipal trolleybus operators, such as Belfast, Manchester or Newcastle, whose respective fleets approximated to 200 vehicles. LT operated 64 trolleybus routes, numbered in a 5xx and 6xx series and covering 494 miles

of service route involving 253 miles of overhead wiring. Trolleybuses were based at 20 depots (detailed in Appendix 5), with a maximum of 1,603 vehicles scheduled for Monday-Friday duties. Many trolleybus routes provided the trunk service between outer areas and the perimeter of Central London, with end-to-end journey times of about 1 hour. Some districts of London were served exclusively by trolleybus, particularly near the Docks and in East London around Plaistow. Route frequencies were high with a 2/3-minute headway being quite usual at peak times.

Trolleybus overhauls were carried out at Charlton Works and Fulwell depot. As Charlton Works was not situated near a trolleybus route, vehicles had to be towed there; in the case of vehicles based at East London depots, this involved a trip across the Thames on the Woolwich Free Ferry. West Ham depot was equipped for repainting trolleybuses.

Buses

Schedules for Central Area buses in 1952 reached their zenith on 6 July when the introduction of new bus routes following the final tramway abandonment — brought forward by three months from the date originally proposed — combined with requirements for Central Area's enhanced summer programme to require a maximum of 6,064 buses on scheduled service for

Above: Some trolleybus routes provided essential outer-London radial links. The 630 ran up to every 3min between West Croydon and Harlesden via Mitcham, Tooting, Wandsworth, Hammersmith and Shepherd's Bush. Leyland/MCCW 'P1' class No 1703 (GGP 703), one of the last batch of standard 'prewar' London trolleybuses (not actually delivered until 1941) speeds past the rural backdrop of Mitcham Common in the autumn of 1952. *Aviation & Transport Photographs, courtesy R. Marshall*

Below: The Leyton and Walthamstow districts were extensively (although not exclusively) served by 11 trolleybus routes. Route 557, operated on a 4min frequency, passed through both areas on its way from Chingford Mount to Liverpool Street station. All-Leyland 'D2' class No 477 (DGY 477) of 1937 is seen at Leyton (Bakers Arms) in the summer of 1952. *C. Carter*

Right: The highest allocation of buses to any individual route in 1952 was on route 12, which on Mondays-Fridays had an allocation of 113 buses (RT/RTL class) from four garages: Elmers End, Nunhead, Shepherd's Bush and Croydon. Sunday working introduced buses from yet two more garages: Peckham and Rye Lane. In its entirety the route between Harlesden and South Croydon via Oxford Circus would have had a through journey time of 2¼ hours; in practice it was worked in two overlapping sections from Harlesden to Dulwich and from Oxford Circus to Croydon, the overlapping section between Oxford Circus and Dulwich enjoying a frequency of up to two minutes. Park Royal-bodied RT1836 (KYY 691) of 1950 is seen passing down Whitehall in July 1952. *G.H.F.Atkins*

Left: In 1952 busy North London route 233 between Finsbury Park and Northumberland Park remained single-deck-operated, with an allocation of 22 Q-class buses from West Green garage, exemplified by Q143 (CLE 166). This 5Q5 variant displays to advantage its true front entrance as it passes Alexandra Palace, part of which was in use at the time as the BBC Television Centre. *G.W.Morant*

Right: Route 223 was unique amongst Central Area routes in 1952 in being officially allocated both single-deckers (T class) and double-deckers (STL and RT classes), from Uxbridge garage. This arose because, whilst double-deckers could work the main service between Ruislip and West Drayton station, they could not pass beneath the bridge in Station Road, West Drayton, for workings to Mill Road, and consequently these journeys had to be worked by single-deckers. T727 (HGF 817), one of a batch of 50 Weymann-bodied AEC Regal O662s delivered in 1946, was photographed in Belmont Road, Uxbridge. *G.Rixon*

Right: Route 101 had the highest individual frequency, the section between Royal Albert Dock and Manor Park being scheduled for a bus every minute at certain times. LPTB-bodied AEC Regent STL743 (BXD 416) of 1935 was one of a large number of London buses rebuilt by Mann Egerton of Norwich in the immediate postwar years. Allocated to Upton Park garage, it is seen working route 101 at East Ham High Street South in July 1952, just four months before withdrawal. *J.C. Gillham*

Non-tramway-replacement bus routes introduced 1952

Date	Route	Termini
16 April	98A	Hounslow Garage–Pinner
14 May	209	Harrow Weald Station–South Harrow Station
14 May	265	East Acton–Chessington Copt Gilders
6 August	79A	Edgware Station–Northolt Airport
22 October	66A	Harold Hill–Romford (extended Monday–Friday peak hours to Newbury Park Station)
22 October	194A	Croydon–Shirley

Bus routes withdrawn 1952

Date	Route	Termini
14 May	65A	Ealing–Chessington Copt Gilders
22 October	166A	Thornton Heath–Old Coulsdon

Right: Brixton was one of a number of Central Area garages with an all-RT allocation. Early in 1952, Weymann-bodied RT3985 (LUC 144) of 1950 is seen in Vauxhall Bridge Road, Victoria, on route 57, which had replaced tram route 20 on 7 January 1951. The 57 via Brixton and allied route 57A via Clapham, while both terminating at Victoria, worked in opposite directions along a common section between Streatham and Tooting. This had caused some passenger confusion as to which direction each route took towards Central London. To try to alleviate this difficulty, '(VIA BRIXTON)' was added to the intermediate blind display. Confused? *Aviation & Transport Photographs, courtesy R. Marshall*

Above: Not all Central Area routes were lengthy or of high frequency, as demonstrated by these two buses seen on layover in the yard at Upminster station on 26 June 1952. On the left is 1948-built, Mann Egerton-bodied Leyland Tiger PS1 TD56 (JXC 249) on route 248, which had a total journey time between its termini at Upminster (Hall Lane) and Cranham (Moor Lane) of 11 minutes. The service was worked by three buses, giving a 10min frequency over the route's main section between Upminster station and Cranham. LPTB-bodied AEC Regent STL1613 (CXX 324) of 1936, meanwhile, represents the entire allocation to route 249, on which it shuttled to and fro every 20 minutes on the 6/7min journey to Corbets Tey. *A. B. Cross, courtesy D. A. Ruddom*

Mondays-Fridays, as detailed in Appendix 6. Original LT policy had been to give route numbers below 200 to double-deck-operated routes, with single-deck-operated routes numbered in a 2xx series. Whilst this still held good for the double-deck routes, from 1942 onwards the distinction with single-deck routes had become blurred following the conversion of certain of these routes to double-deck operation, such that by mid-1952 only 35 out of 53 daytime bus routes in the 2xx series remained single-deck-operated. Higher route numbers — 285-298 — were allocated to Night Bus services, which were all double-deck-operated. A total of 43 routes, including Sunday variants, worked right across Central London via the West End or City giving lengthy terminus-to-terminus journey times of about 1½ hours. Many trunk routes enjoyed a scheduled peak-hour frequency of 2/3 minutes, and the combination of several routes along the same section of road really did lead to the spectacle of an oncoming bus being in sight almost all the time. As might be expected, the most intensively-served locations were on traffic arteries leading to the West End. During 1952 Trafalgar Square held the record, with 758 buses per hour scheduled to pass through at Monday-Friday peak times — a bus every five seconds!

Not far behind came Hyde Park Corner, with 715 buses per hour at Monday-Friday peaks. Other heavily-bussed spots were Piccadilly Circus, Oxford Circus and Marble Arch, with Monday-Friday peaktime schedules of respectively 646, 576 and 562 buses per hour.

Hornchurch garage, on the outer fringes of the Central Area, enjoyed a notable distinction at the beginning of 1952. With amongst the greatest variety of vehicle types allocated, with four classes of double-decker (STL, G, RTL and SRT) and two classes of single-decker (T and TD), it worked 16 different routes — the most by any single garage. But by 1952 Hornchurch was atypical of a Central Area bus garage. The relentless progress of LT's standardisation programme was evidenced by the fact that, by mid-year, 25 garages were stocked entirely with RT-family vehicles. The overwhelming bias of many other garages in favour of the RT family was leavened only by the allocation of a few remaining STL-class double-deckers or of elderly single-deckers.

The increase in the number of Central Area bus routes from a total of 265 at 1 January 1952 to 282 at 31 December 1952 was largely attributable to the introduction of tramway-replacement bus routes, which

Above: Joint operation of the 359 (Aylesbury–Amersham) by LT and Eastern National commenced on 29 September 1942, when existing EN route 107 (Aylesbury–Great Missenden) was extended to Amersham, partially to compensate for the withdrawal of Green Line route 35 (Aylesbury–London) due to wartime exigencies. Eastern National's share of operation transferred to United Counties on 1 May 1952, when the former's entire Midland section centred on Bedford passed to the Northampton-based operator. For a while, LT used surplus lowbridge RLH-class buses, which better matched the lowbridge ECW-bodied Bristol K double-deckers used by United Counties, although, as this view of RT3889 (LLU 688) on layover at Kingsbury Square, Aylesbury, emphasises, the route was not subject to any lowbridge constraint. *R.H.G. Simpson*

PERIMETER OF THE COUNTRY AREA

London Transport's Country Area spanned 65 miles from its northernmost point to its southern extremity.

Above: Seen at Hertford bus station, 1934-built STL411 (AXM 673) works route 331 bound for Buntingford, one of the most northerly points served by LT. The northernmost point reached in 1952 was Letchworth on route 384, also from Hertford. *G.W. Morant*

Left: The most southerly point reached by LT was Horham Carfax, where 1935-built STL1011 (BLH 870) is seen on 1 September 1952 on a short working of route 434 to Roffey Corner. This was effectively a Horsham town service, and provided a combined 20min frequency with route 32 of Basil Williams' Hants & Sussex. *M.J. Dryhurst*

are detailed in subsequent chapters. However, a few route alterations were unconnected with that programme and are detailed on page 16. Perhaps most interesting was the introduction of routes 79A and 98A, intended to give improved services to Northolt Airport, off Western Avenue, for in 1952 this, as with the burgeoning London Airport at Heath Row, was used by civil airlines.

Country Bus & Coach Department

This Department, administered from Bell Street, Reigate, was responsible for operating green-liveried buses in the Country Area, as well as Green Line coaches. The Country Area was akin to a circle with a hole punched out of the middle wherein Central Road Services operated. Despite much interface between Country Bus and Central routes in outer London, the two Departments operated virtually as separate businesses, with no joint operation of services. Although much smaller than

Central Road Services in terms of vehicles operated, on a national scale Country Bus & Coach ranked as one of Britain's largest non-municipal provincial operators. In 1952 only Bristol Tramways and Crosville, with around 1,300 vehicles each, were of comparable size, whilst Midland Red, with about 1,700 vehicles, was the only larger non-municipal provincial operator.

The Country Area, divided almost equally by the River Thames, split naturally into Northern and Southern Areas. Bus routes in the Northern Area, formed by an arc swinging westwards from Grays/Tilbury to High Wycombe/Uxbridge, were numbered in a 3xx series. Those in the Southern Area, defined by the same arc sweeping eastwards to complete a circle on the Thames Estuary at Gravesend, were numbered in a 4xx series. The Estuary, across which no road-vehicle crossing was possible east of the Woolwich Free Ferry, acted as a natural barrier to physical connection between Northern and Southern Area bus routes east of London. On

Below: Hemel Hempstead-based RT612 (HLX 429) is seen on layover on route 302, having reversed into the Windmill Road terminus off Longlands, Adeyfield. Behind the bus, stacks of bricks bear witness to the ongoing development programme in Hemel Hempstead New Town. *The Omnibus Society*

Above: The rich variety of vehicle types operated by the Country Bus & Coach Department is well demonstrated in this view taken at Dorking garage in June 1952. Normal-control, one-man-operated Leyland Cub C47 (BXD 672) stands across the yard from T599 (EYK 234), a 10T10 AEC Regal Green Line coach recently downgraded to bus duties. The nearest of the three RTs, RT3516 (MLL 826), was new into LT stock only the previous month, whilst the other two, RT3124/5 (KXW 233/4), date from 1950. RT3125 has blinds set for a relief working on Green Line route 714, Green Line duties being quite a common task for double-deckers in 1952. *M.J.Dryhurst*

the western side of the Country Area, only three bus routes — 335 (Watford–Windsor), 353 (Berkhamstead–Windsor) and 441 (High Wycombe–Staines) — crossed between the two areas. Of these, the 335 provided the sole example of route working shared between Northern and Southern Area garages, with Watford High Street and Windsor each providing four RT-class double-deckers. The Country Area provided four examples (shown below) of rare joint workings between London Transport and other operators, two such being independents and two being BTC-controlled Tilling Group companies.

The Green Line network comprised limited-stop bus routes numbered in a 7xx series. Intended for use by medium- to long-distance travellers, these discouraged short-distance traffic by charging premium fares. Many Green Line services linked country termini on different sides of the Metropolis, with routeing through Central London; such routes had through journey times in the order of three hours. Green Line routes operated to a high frequency, usually every 30 minutes, seven days a week.

As may be seen from Appendix 7, the 30 Country Bus & Coach garages were, on average, much smaller in terms of allocation and capacity than their Central counterparts. Smallest of all was Tunbridge Wells, a point well outside the LPTA to which London Transport enjoyed running rights under the terms of the 1933 Act, where 8 RF-class coaches were scheduled for Green Line route 704 to Windsor. Hitchin was not much larger, with a building too low to accommodate double-deck buses. This caused a problem when the garage's first two RT-class double-deckers were allocated on 24 September 1952 for Stevenage New Town services 392/392A, only resolved by finding an open parking space for them. A few garages, such as Leatherhead, St Albans and Windsor, held larger allocations. On 11 June 1952 the first new postwar Country garage opened at Garston. This facility replaced Watford Leavesden Road garage, as well as absorbing some workings from Watford High Street.

The thrust of expansion in the Country Bus & Coach Department was associated with the growing New Towns, as a schedule (opposite) of new services and developments in 1952 details.

Route No	Termini	Operated jointly with
316	Hemel Hempstead–Chesham	J. R. G. Dell (t/a Rover Bus Service)
326/326A	High Wycombe town services	Thames Valley Traction Co Ltd
359	Amersham–Aylesbury	Eastern National Omnibus Co Ltd (operation transferred to United Counties Omnibus Co Ltd with effect 1 May 1952)
448	Guildford–Peaslake	Tillingbourne Valley Services Ltd

Country Bus & Coach Department principal route developments 1952

Date	Route	Description
20 February	302	Extended within Hemel Hempstead New Town to Adeyfield (Longlands).
20 February	396	First bus service introduced in Harlow New Town (renumbered 396A from 24 September 1952 to avoid confusion with main 396 route (Epping–Harlow–Bishop's Stortford).
5 March	312/345/346/346A/347	Enhanced services to Oxhey Estate, Watford. 346A and 347 were new routes.
26 March	330	Re-routed to serve Longmead area in Hatfield New Town.
26 March	392	First bus service introduced in Stevenage New Town to Monks Wood.
30 April	(various)	Revision to routes in Grays area to improve services to Aveley LCC Estate
14 May	420	New route introduced between Woking and Sheerwater LCC Estate (extended from Sheerwater to West Byfleet from 15 Oct 1952).
11 June	(various)	Route changes associated with opening of new Garston garage, including extensions to new housing developments.
11 June	473	New route introduced between Edenbridge and Horsham via East Grinstead and Crawley New Town
11 June	498	New route introduced Gravesend–Coldharbour Estate.
24 September	392A	Second bus service introduced in Stevenage New Town to Bedworth.
12 November	301C/302/316	First extension of selected journeys to Maylands Avenue Industrial Area in Hemel Hempstead New Town.
3 December	325/391A	Extended in St Albans to Cottonmill Estate/New Greens Estate respectively.
3 December	717	Diverted to serve Sheerwater LCC Estate.
17 December	314A	New route introduced in Hemel Hempstead New Town to Bennetts End.

Below: The Country Bus & Coach Department outstationed only two buses away from a main garage overnight. One was at Holmbury St Mary for route 412, whilst the other, illustrated here, was at Loudwater for route 336A. Although this scene has a timeless quality and could easily date from the 1930s, the 336A, providing a link between the exclusive Loudwater Estate and Rickmansworth LT station, was a relatively new operation for LT, which took over the service from previous operator Land & Estates on 6 June 1950. LT substituted a C-class one-man-operated Leyland Cub, like C60 (BXD 685) seen here, for the former operator's Dennis Ace. *The Omnibus Society*

2

All Change for Victoria and Grove Park

THE first of their six visits to London Transport operations in 1952 required Richard Forall and John Ryder to make an early-morning journey up to the capital from Reading on Saturday 5 January. They wanted to take this last opportunity to travel on some of the tram routes which would be replaced by buses the next day under Stage 6 of Operation Tramaway, destined to be the largest conversion so far in London's tramway-replacement programme, and in which 109 scheduled tram workings would be replaced by 105 buses. Emerging from Victoria Coach Station just after 9am, they were pleased at the prospect of a dry day for, although cloudy, the sky showed no sign of rain. It was not too cold either, considering the time of year. Walking down Buckingham Palace Road, they noticed busy Green Line coach activity on Eccleston Bridge. Further along, after turning right into the forecourt of

Victoria station, they became intrigued by the hive of activity at the London Transport bus terminal in front of the station. Buses were arriving and departing at an average of every 15 seconds, on a wide variety of routes. Studying the timetables, they were amazed at how far it was possible to travel by bus from Victoria. Far-flung corners of the Central Area were accessible depending on day and time of day: route 10 ran out as far as Abridge in Essex in the evenings and on Saturday afternoons; on Saturdays South Mimms could be reached in 1hr 34min using route 29.

After a while Richard and John turned the corner into Vauxhall Bridge Road. Drinking 2d cups of tea bought from the refreshment bar under the clock tower, they watched operations at the tram terminal. John, who had passed through Victoria in early 1950 during his RAF days, noticed how much reduced tramway activity was

Below: Eccleston Bridge was the principal Central London interchange point for Green Line services and was served by 11 routes. Here, the ever-present inspectors supervise 1949 Cravens-bodied RT1424 (JXC 187), which has just unloaded after a relief journey on route 704 from Windsor, where the bus was based. At the back of the shelter may be seen an exemplary display of route information, including timetables and a map representative of the high standards of roadside information provided by London Transport in 1952. The 120 Cravens-bodied RTs, built in 1948/9, featured non-standard bodywork which was not interchangable with that of other suppliers to LT. *G.H.F.Atkins*

compared with then. At that earlier date, before Operation Tramaway had started, Victoria had been one of the busiest inner-London tram terminals, served by seven routes. Now tram operations were reduced to just daily route 54 to Grove Park and weekdays-only route 78 to West Norwood. Walking further down Vauxhall Bridge Road, the friends were delighted to find the Ian Allan bookshop at No 282. Both had bought copies of a new magazine for bus enthusiasts, titled *Buses Illustrated*, when it was first published in 1949. Getting hold of subsequent issues had proved difficult, since the problems experienced by the British economy in the early postwar years had caused shortages of many basic materials, including paper. Richard had managed to buy a copy of issue No 8 in a local newsagent's in August 1951, but had not seen any further issues. Entering the shop and browsing around, they were pleased to see a pile of *Buses Illustrated* No 9 on display. Each bought a copy along with copies of Ian Allan's *ABC London Transport Buses and Coaches* and the separate *ABC London Transport Trams and Trolleybuses*. Whilst giving them their change the manager of the shop introduced himself as Prince Marshall, explaining that he too was a keen transport enthusiast and would be riding the tram routes later in the afternoon once the shop closed.

Above: The farthest point reached by a Central Area bus from Victoria was Hornchurch station, almost two hours' travelling-time distant, on selected peak-hour journeys of route 25. The main service operated from Victoria to Becontree Heath, 1½ hours distant, every 2-4 minutes on weekdays, and required an allocation of 89 double-deckers. Of these, 81 were RTs from Forest Gate garage, these being assisted by eight RTLs from Clay Hall. An example of the former, 1948-built RT438 (HLX 255), passes West Ham Municipal Baths in Romford Road. *A.B.Cross*

'I wonder if Ian Allan will be able to keep *Buses Illustrated* going?' Richard mused aloud as they left the shop. 'I do hope so.'

Below: 'E/3'-class tramcar No 1991, with blind set for a journey to West Norwood on route 78, stands at Victoria's tram terminus at the north end of Vauxhall Bridge Road on 5 January 1952. RT2486 (KXW 115), squeezing by to the left of the tram, is working a journey on 2-4min-frequency route 2 from Crystal Palace to Golders Green. Ahead, another RT bus has strayed onto the tram track, preventing 1991 from travelling the final few yards to the official stop. *J.C.Gillham*

Above: 'E/3'-class car No 171, originally owned by Leyton Corporation, heads southwards from Lambeth Road into Stockwell Road on 5 January 1952. Behind the car, one of Merton garage's utility Daimlers turns right to follow route 88 into Clapham Road — still with tram tracks *in situ*, one year after the tram routes concerned are converted to bus operation. *C. Carter*

Tram route 78: Victoria–West Norwood

Making their way back to the tram terminal at around 10.30am, the pair boarded tramcar No 171 waiting to depart on route 78. Passing the rear controls, John followed Richard up the narrow spiral stairway to the top deck, where they made for an empty front seat, reversing the seat-back to suit the car's new direction of travel. Richard explained to John that the tramcars which comprised London Transport's fleet on its formation in 1933 had come from various predecessors. The greatest number were originally in the London County Council Tramways fleet, whilst others had originated with company fleets operated by Metropolitan Electric Tramways, South Metropolitan Electric Tramways and London United Tramways. Yet others had previously been owned by the municipalities at Bexley, Croydon, East Ham, Erith, Ilford, Leyton, Walthamstow and West Ham. At the beginning of 1952 about two thirds of London's 378 remaining tramcars were of London County Council origin. Former municipal cars from the fleets of Croydon, East Ham, Leyton, Walthamstow and West Ham also remained in use, although the surviving Croydon and Walthamstow cars would be withdrawn that day.

At 10.32am the pair felt a slight jolt as 171 set off down a quiet Vauxhall Bridge Road, allowing the motorman quickly to notch up the controller until 171 hit top speed as it approached Vauxhall Bridge. The conductor, having come upstairs to collect the fares, had to cling on to a seat stanchion as 171 lurched across the track junction at Vauxhall where route 78 turned southwards, separating from the Camberwell-bound 54 route. In splendid isolation 171 sped along South Lambeth Road and into Stockwell. On entering Brixton, route 78 was joined from the north by tram route 33, one of the two remaining Kingsway Subway routes which worked from Manor House to West Norwood. Brixton was a hive of busy Saturday-morning shopping activity, its Market attracting good passenger loadings for the two tram and many bus routes passing through.

With a near-capacity load, 171 reached Brixton's change-pit at Effra Road. Immediately in front of 171, 'E/3' car No 1938 on route 33 was already at the change-pit. The pair watched, fascinated, as 1938's conductor raised the trolley pole to the overhead wire, after which the car moved slowly forward until they saw the 'plough' shoot out from underneath the tram to come to rest along the curved conduit exit slot. Now set up for overhead-wire operation, 1938 sped away, after which 171 inched onto the change-pit for similar treatment. About one minute later, 171 set off again past Brockwell Park and towards Herne Hill, where it caught

Above: 'E/3'-class car No 1940 heads southwards through Brixton towards both the camera and West Norwood on Kingsway Subway route 33. Across the wide A23 Brixton Road, RT4018 (LUC 177) works the lengthy 159 route from West Hampstead to South Croydon via Oxford Circus. *C. Carter*

up with car 1938 which had been delayed picking up passengers along Dulwich Road. At the right-hand turn into Norwood Road, tramway tracks used by route 48 joined from the north. Now in convoy, 1938 and 171 went through Tulse Hill and passed Norwood tram depot before approaching the West Norwood terminus at the 'Thurlow Arms' at 11.05am. Here 171 stopped short of the terminal to allow 1938 to complete its crossover move onto the return track. Richard and John alighted from 171 and spent a while near the terminal, watching tram arrivals and departures every two or three minutes on routes 33, 48 and 78. There was a lot of bus activity too, with frequent sightings of RT- and RTL-class double-deckers on routes 2, 68 and 196. Richard and John set off along Knights Hill and soon came to Norwood bus garage. Glancing inside, they saw that it was largely empty, as would be expected on a Saturday. Parked-up in a far corner was a utility Guy Arab used for driver training and sporting L-plates.

Tram route 48: West Norwood–Southwark

About one hour later, when heading back towards the tram terminal, Richard and John saw 'E/3'-class car 1993 about to depart on route 48. Clearly ready to set off, the conductor looked from the platform for any last passengers, saw them running and waited until they

were aboard before ringing the bell. Route 48 retraced their earlier journey as far as Herne Hill, where, after the railway bridge, the roads followed by route 48 became noticeably narrower and involved an unusual section of single-track, one-way-system working along Milkwood Road. Approaching Loughborough Junction, 1993 was stopped by a signal just before another section of single track. After waiting about 30 seconds they saw car 1996 approaching on the single track, bound for West Norwood. This working was necessary because the left-hand turn from Coldharbour Lane into Herne Road was so tight that West Norwood-bound cars had to use a special crossover to gain access to the 'up' track to complete the manœuvre. Car 1996 completed its turn, the signal changed and 1993 was able to set off again. Just before reaching Denmark Hill there was a delay at the Coldharbour Lane change-pit whilst the plough was inserted and trolley pole lowered before 1993 could continue.

Reaching Camberwell Green, route 48 crossed the tracks of tram routes 40, 54 and 72 and was joined by the other Kingsway Subway route 35 (Forest Hill–Highgate). A host of bus routes were encountered here, many of which had allocations from the two large neighbouring bus garages at Camberwell and Walworth. The latter had been extensively rebuilt to repair wartime bomb damage and again during its conversion from

SOUTHWARK BRIDGE

Originally, Southwark tram terminus had been to the north of Southwark Bridge — a rare tramway incursion into the City of London. However, bomb damage sustained in 1941 forced the terminus to be moved southwards onto Southwark Bridge itself, and consequently two 'temporary' military Bailey Bridges were erected to allow road traffic to continue across the bridge. These arrangements continued into 1952.

Right: Brixton-based RT3843 (LLU 642) heads southwards out of the City across the Bailey Bridge, with the spire of St Michael Paternoster Royal Church — where Dick Whittington is buried — in the background. Bus route 95 replaced tram route 10 with effect from 7 January 1951 as part of Stage 2 of Operation Tramaway.
V.C. Jones/Ian Allan Library

Left: 'E/3'-class car No 1992 stands on Southwark Bridge with the Bailey Bridge visible to the right. Enthusiasts gather in this view taken on 5 January 1952. *G.W. Morant*

Right: The crew chalk slogans on 1927-built former Walthamstow Corporation 'E/1' car No 2043 prior to its working the last journey on route 52 to Grove Park. All remaining ex-Walthamstow cars were withdrawn after 5 January 1952.
V.C. Jones/Ian Allan Library

tram to bus operation, its final tram routes having been withdrawn only on 6 October 1951. At the top of Walworth Road they reached the major traffic intersection at Elephant & Castle, around which bomb-damaged sites still bore silent testimony to the devastation inflicted on London during the Blitz. Crossing the tracks used by the Abbey Wood tram routes 36/38 as well as the 74 from Blackfriars to Grove Park (the latter destined also to be withdrawn that day), 1993 went along Newington Causeway into Borough. Passing great warehouses and other commercial premises, 1993 reached the terminus at Southwark Bridge, where Richard and John alighted.

Now, at nearly 1pm, the terminus was a hive of activity. The working week usually included Saturday mornings, so that at this time many City workers were heading home on the trams. As well as route 48, trams were leaving every few minutes on routes 46 to Woolwich and 52 to Grove Park. Needing some sustenance, the pair crossed the bridge to the City side, finding a kiosk open near Cannon Street station. Suitably refreshed, they returned to Southwark Bridge to find that a considerable number of enthusiasts had gathered. Some faces were familiar to them from Southern Counties Touring Society visits and, recognising Victor Jones, the well-known transport photographer, they chatted with him for a few minutes.

Tram route 52: Southwark–Grove Park

Richard and John squeezed onto tram 2043, which was full to capacity, mostly with enthusiasts. Soon after, at

2.08pm (eight minutes late), 2043 set off, heading down the Old Kent Road — until close of service that day the only principal inner-London thoroughfare with all its tram routes intact from prewar days — also served by tram routes 36, 38, 46 and 74 (and night route 5) towards New Cross. Here the convergence of the A2 and A20 trunk roads, carrying much traffic to South East London and Kent, created a major bottleneck, so that congestion was commonplace. No 2043 joined a queue of trams inching their way along New Cross Road past the tram depot which was the largest in London, being capable of accommodating 250 cars. A convoy of army lorries carrying troops was also caught up in the traffic.

'I wonder where all those soldiers are off to?' pondered John.

'Probably heading for the Docks and a troopship out to Korea,' replied Richard.

Towards the 'Marquis of Granby' junction, 2043 stopped at the tail end of a line of trams. What was amiss became clear a few minutes later when broken-down car 300 passed by on the parallel track, being pushed by a Karrier breakdown wagon. The queue eased, and, finally clearing New Cross, 2043 notched up speed along Lewisham Way and down Loampit Vale. After passing through Lewisham 2043 headed south through Catford and down Bromley Road past the massive Catford bus garage. Richard explained that the letter 'T' in the garage code (TL) indicated that it had once been used by Thomas Tilling Ltd, a pioneer London bus operator. Turning into Downham Way, the pair encountered their third change-pit working of the day, when the trolley pole was positioned and the

A BIT OF BOVVER DAHN NEW CROSS

**Former West Ham 'E/1'-class car No 300 broke down in New Cross
on 5 January 1952, leading to temporary disruption to other tram routes.**

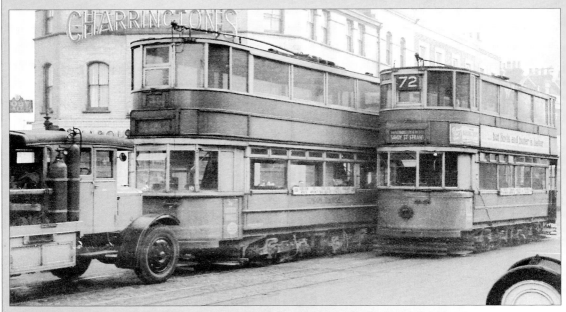

Above: Karrier breakdown wagon No 176K pushes 300 from New Cross into Lewisham Way past 'The Marquis of Granby'
to gain a crossover further down the track. *G.W.Morant*

Below: Route 52 should have turned right along the tracks into Lewisham Way but was prevented from so doing by the broken-down car. To
alleviate a bottleneck that had built up in New Cross, cars on routes 35, 46, 52, 54, 72 and 74 were forced to continue along the 'wrong' track in
New Cross Road towards Greenwich, normally used by routes 36, 38 and 40 only. The policeman on point duty is kept busy by the situation as
unique car No 2, rebuilt from a damaged car to an experimental modern style in 1933, heads 'off route' along New Cross Road. *G.W.Morant*

Left: Route 74, bound for Grove Park via Brockley, should also have turned right into Lewisham Way. Former Croydon Corporation 'E/1'-class car No 395 already has its blinds set for a return journey to Blackfriars, indicating that this was probably a short working to New Cross which, when it gained a crossover, would return on the parallel track. All the surviving ex-Croydon tramcars were withdrawn after 5 January 1952. Plumstead garage's RTL167 (KGK 831) squeezes by on the inside on its 1½hr route 53A journey from Camden Town to Plumstead Common. *G.W.Morant*

Above: Having made a crossover, the Karrier breakdown wagon has had to manœuvre to push car 300 from the opposite end. The convoy is seen here heading back into New Cross, with members of the breakdown gang standing on the platform. Inverted sideboards show that 300 is out of service, not that any intending passengers would have been left in much doubt in that respect, judging by the progress of this procession. *G.W.Morant*

Right: Having reached the tracks outside New Cross depot, the Karrier has to change pushing ends yet again to ease 300 through the more westerly entrance to the depot. *G.W.Morant*

Above: 'E/1'-class car No 1387, dating from 1910, loads at Downham Way, Grove Park. This car was one of 154 tramcars reconditioned in 1935/6. Improvements included new upholstered seating in the upper saloon, enhanced décor and fittings and the provision of recessed roller-blind destination displays. *C. Carter*

plough removed. With power from the overhead wire, 2043 swept up Downham Way along the last tramway extension to have been introduced by the London County Council, in 1928 in conjunction with that authority's simultaneous development of a low-density housing estate. Reaching the Grove Park terminus at 3.02pm, Richard and John left 2043 which shortly thereafter set off on the final route 52 working back to New Cross depot.

Tram route 54: Grove Park–Victoria

Tram routes 54 to Victoria and 74 to Blackfriars also served Grove Park. Richard and John watched the activity at the terminal for a while before boarding rebuilt 'E/1' car No 1387 for a 3.55pm departure on route 54. For 8d each they bought tickets through to Victoria and settled down for an hour-long journey. Re-tracing their outward journey as far as New Cross Gate, route 54 then headed for Peckham. Here the car passed Peckham bus garage as well as a new garage at Rye Lane (off Peckham High Street) converted from a former tramway permanent-way depot, where they

glimpsed a host of RT-class buses ready to take up tramway-replacement duties the next day. Travelling through Camberwell and then past The Oval cricket ground, route 54 met up with tram route 78 at Vauxhall before crossing Vauxhall Bridge and heading for Victoria, where it arrived at 4.57pm.

Unfortunately, prior commitments prevented the two friends from witnessing the last trams later that evening; John had to return to Reading whilst Richard stayed with friends in London over the weekend. They subsequently learned that the final tram departures from Victoria had been worked by 'E/3'-class cars No 1998 on route 78 and — the last car of all — No 1920 on route 54.

Replacement bus routes

An early start on Monday 7 January saw Richard in a still-dark Victoria at about 7am and feeling somewhat confused, as there was no sign of any replacement bus routes anywhere near the now-deserted tram terminal. To make matters worse, the welcoming kiosk where he and John had got a cup of tea last Saturday seemed to have closed along with the trams. Walking further down

Above: One distinct disadvantage to passengers caused by the tramway conversion programme at Victoria was the removal of the terminus an appreciable distance southwards, down Vauxhall Bridge Road — further from the main-line and Underground railway stations as well as many other connecting bus routes, all of which were objectives for many passengers. The reason was to enable buses on tram-replacement routes to execute a U-turn at the new terminus, which was situated in a wider part of Vauxhall Bridge Road. Here, Rye Lane garage's RT2735 (LYR 719) performs this manœuvre whilst RT3347 (LYR 566) waits its turn to follow. The sign above the Ian Allan bookshop may be seen a little beyond the roof of the first car, whilst the Cameo Hotel, where Richard Forall and John Ryder stayed overnight on 1 May 1952, is just to the right. *C. Carter*

Below: Weymann-bodied RT3385 (LYR 604) waits just short of the final stop in Downham Way, Grove Park. As yet unsullied by advertisements, this pristine bus was one of 77 new RTs included in Rye Lane's allocation of 87 such buses when it first opened for service on 6 January 1952. *C. F. Klapper/The Omnibus Society*

Vauxhall Bridge Road, he came across the terminal for new bus routes 69 and 178 near the Ian Allan bookshop just as RT3390 pulled up on the 69. Richard boarded and got an upstairs front seat. A minute later the conductor rang the bell and the bus set off. Richard felt the RT accelerate away smoothly as the driver swiftly progressed through the preselector gearbox. The bus had that extra-clean feeling of a brand-new vehicle, a slight scent of fresh paint complementing the sense of airiness and lightness which contrasted markedly with his recollections of the reverse journey on tram route 54 just two days earlier. The conductor came upstairs to collect his fare. As the journey was against the flow of the rush hour, there were not many passengers and RT3390 made good progress. The conductor chatted with Richard, telling him that Rye Lane garage's take-up of the former tram routes had gone very smoothly.

'London Transport plan everything to the last detail,' he said with a sense of pride.

Reaching Grove Park about an hour later, Richard left the AEC and inspected the terminal arrangements. At this time of day it was very busy with school children and workers using the new bus routes. An inspector noticed Richard's interest and told him that he, along with three colleagues, had been sent to the area to make sure passengers understood the changes and caught the right bus. Richard recalled the conductor's earlier remarks and had to agree; London Transport was indeed very thorough.

Wishing to try a different route back, Richard caught the last morning inward-bound journey on rush-hour-only route 149, bound for Cannon Street at 8.43am. Another new bus, RT3398, carried him on his journey, which retraced former tram route 52 along which he had travelled just two days previously. The rush hour was easing, so that RT3398 made steady progress, continuing over Southwark Bridge beyond the tram terminus still in use for cars on route 46 to Woolwich and on to its own terminus at Cannon Street station.

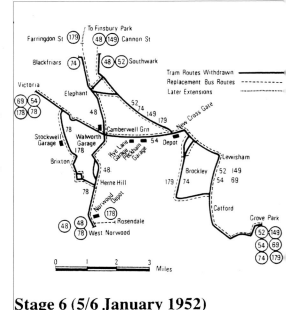

Stage 6 (5/6 January 1952)

Richard now needed to get to Victoria Coach Station as quickly as possible, since he hoped to catch the 10.30am Thames Valley route B departure for Reading to get him back in time for work in the afternoon. Walking briskly from Dowgate Hill, he reached the route 11 bus stop in Queen Victoria Street just as RTW225 pulled up. Travelling past St Paul's Cathedral, up Fleet Street and along the Strand, through Trafalgar Square, down Whitehall past the entrance to Downing Street, and then past the Houses of Parliament and Westminster Abbey — almost a sightseeing tour of London — the 11 reached Victoria in time for Richard to make his connection.

Operation Tramaway Stage 6 (5/6 January 1952)

Tram routes withdrawn		Replacement bus routes	
48	West Norwood–Southwark Bridge	48	West Norwood–Cannon Street (Weekdays) Norwood Garage–Elephant (Sundays)
52	Grove Park–Southwark Bridge (Weekday peak hours only)	149	Grove Park–Cannon Street (Weekday peak hours only)
54	Grove Park–Victoria	69	Grove Park–Victoria (also some augmentation of 36/36A)
74	Grove Park–Blackfriars	179	Grove Park–Farringdon Street (Weekdays) Grove Park–Elephant (Sundays)
78	West Norwood–Victoria (Weekdays only)	178	West Norwood–Victoria (Weekdays only)
5	Savoy Street–Downham (All night — Saturday night/ Sunday morning excepted)	285	Charing Cross (LT station)–Downham (All night, with journeys to Grove Park — Saturday night/Sunday morning excepted)

Above: The bus stand situated east of the railway line in Baring Road, Grove Park, provided the sole example of a purpose-built bus stand constructed during the entire postwar tramway-abandonment programme. Built to LT's high standards of the period, it was well equipped, including the provision of a small canteen, supervisor's office and staff toilets. Four RTs on tram-replacement routes are seen on layover. Whilst terminating journeys were allowed to set down passengers here, boarding was not permitted, so intending passengers still had to catch their bus to the west of the railway line, in Downham Way. *C. Carter*

Journey schedule

Saturday 5 January 1952

Terminus	Dep/Arr	Route No	Vehicle	Depot Allocation	Fare
Victoria Station	10.32am	Tram 78	'E/3' 171 *	Norwood	5d
West Norwood	11.05am				
West Norwood	12.08pm	Tram 48	'E/3' 1993	Norwood	5d
Southwark Bridge	12.46pm				
Southwark Bridge	2.08pm	Tram 52	'E/1' 2043 §	New Cross	8d
Grove Park Station	3.02pm				
Grove Park Station	3.55pm	Tram 54	'E/1R' 1387	New Cross	8d
Victoria Station	4.57pm				

* ex-Leyton   § ex-Walthamstow

Journey schedule

Monday 7 January 1952

Terminus	Dep/Arr	Route No	Vehicle	Garage Allocation	Fare
Victoria (Vauxhall Bridge Rd)	7.15am	Bus 69	RT3390	RL	8d
Grove Park Station	8.16am				
Grove Park Station	8.34am	Bus 149	RT3398	RL	8d
Cannon Street Station	9.41am				
Mansion House Stn	9.52am	Bus 11	RTW225	D	4d
Victoria LT Station	10.09am				

Above: 'HR/2'-class car No 132 waits at Archway terminus on 5 April 1952. This type was designed for use on hilly routes (hence the 'HR' code), being fitted with four motors instead of the usual two. The batch of 59 to which No 132 belonged, built in 1931 by Hurst Nelson, were intended for use on conduit routes only, so were not equipped with trolley poles. By 1952 this restricted their use on through workings to route 35 — the sole surviving all-conduit route. The trolleybus wires continuing behind the tram up Highgate Hill to Highgate Village were used by route 611, which was converted from tramway operation on 6 December 1939. *C. Carter*

Below: 'E/3'-class car No 1995 heads southwards from Islington High Street (the left-hand side of the same road being known as Upper Street). The wide thoroughfare had developed over many centuries' use when The Angel was the nearest staging-post to London on the Great North Road. *J. C. Gillham*

— 3 —

Down the Spout

SATURDAY 5 April 1952 would be the last on which trams would run through the Kingsway Subway, dubbed 'The Spout'. Richard and John wanted to take this last opportunity to ride the two remaining Subway tram routes. Catching an early train from Reading, the pair reached Paddington station just after 9.00am. Having walked to the bus stop in Praed Street, they waited for a minute or two until RTL348 arrived on route 27A to Highgate Archway. They boarded and got an upstairs seat. The Leyland Titan made good time along Marylebone Road and into Euston Road. Turning left into Hampstead Road, route 27A travelled under the wires of the Tottenham Court Road trolleybus routes. After passing through Camden Town and then into Kentish Town, the pair noticed trolleybus wires leading off to the left along Highgate Road, used by the Parliament Hill Fields routes. Further overhead, as well as conduit tram tracks, were encountered at Archway terminus, where they alighted. John remembered that Archway's name originated from an arch used in the construction of what became known as Archway Road, built as long ago as

1808 to divert the Great North Road around Highgate Hill. Today they watched the frequent passage of trolleybuses along these same ancient roads. There was plenty of bus activity too; one particularly interesting route was the single-deck-operated 210 from Golders Green to Finsbury Park, its five-minute headway maintained by a mix of prewar AEC 'Q' types and postwar TD-class Leyland Tiger PS1s.

Knowing that time would be at a premium, since they had to return home in the late afternoon, they boarded 'HR/2'-class tramcar No 132 waiting at the stub terminus at the bottom of Highgate Hill. At 10.02am the tram set off for Forest Hill on route 35, and proceeded to make good time down Holloway Road to the 'Nag's Head'. From here onwards there were queues of passengers, both for route 35 and for the various trolleybuses also serving this road. 'J1'-class trolleybus No 920, on lengthy route 609 (Barnet–Moorgate), was just in front of No 132. The two vehicles, the tram powered from the conduit and the trolleybus from overhead wires, then leap-frogged each other down the wide section of Holloway Road, between them coping with passengers,

Left: No 1992, another 'E/3', waits at Manor House. As well as tram route 33, nine trolleybus routes served Manor House, resulting in 270 trolleybus movements per hour on Saturday mornings. Motor buses were in a distinct minority; apart from Green Line routes 715 and 718, the only LT bus routes to serve Manor House were the 29 — a haunt of independent operators before the 1933 Act — and night route 290. *C. Carter*

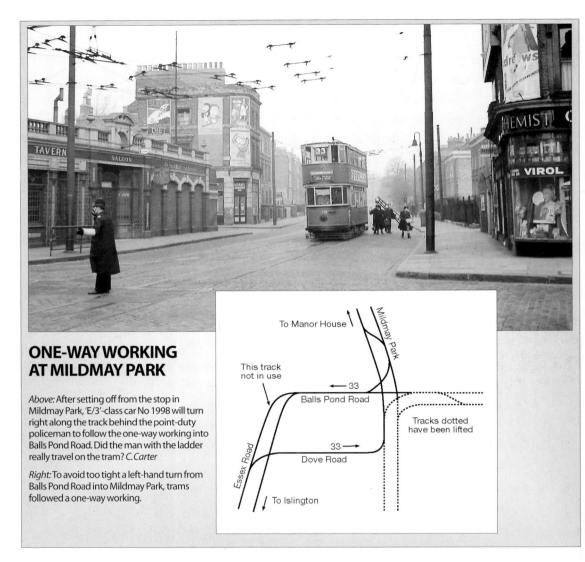

ONE-WAY WORKING AT MILDMAY PARK

Above: After setting off from the stop in Mildmay Park, 'E/3'-class car No 1998 will turn right along the track behind the point-duty policeman to follow the one-way working into Balls Pond Road. Did the man with the ladder really travel on the tram? *C. Carter*

Right: To avoid too tight a left-hand turn from Balls Pond Road into Mildmay Park, trams followed a one-way working.

In diagram:

To Manor House

Mildmay Park

This track not in use

← 33

Balls Pond Road

Tracks dotted have been lifted

Essex Road

33 →

Dove Road

To Islington

---

until pulling up in convoy at Islington Green. Richard and John alighted and, as both were feeling thirsty, scouted around for a café, by chance discovering that the hostelry at The Angel — a name familiar from Underground maps — was now converted into a Lyons Corner House. After drinking welcome cups of coffee the duo left The Angel and walked to the northbound tram stop in Upper Street. Soon 'E/3'-class car No 1948 arrived on route 33 to Manor House, and they boarded. Travelling up Essex Road, 1948 negotiated the one-way tram working at Balls Pond Road before passing through Newington Green to Manor House terminus at the junction of Green Lane and Seven Sisters Road. After alighting there, Richard and John watched the transport scene with fascination, soon realising that Manor House had one of the highest concentrations of electrically-powered road passenger transport in London.

Through the Kingsway Subway

After half an hour or so observing the almost continual procession of trolleybuses, Richard and John boarded 'E/3'-class car No 1992, which set off southwards at 11.35am. Retracing their earlier journey as far as Islington, 1992 then encountered a traffic jam at the busy Angel crossroads. Despite traffic-light control, it took several minutes for 1992 to cross Pentonville Road. Once this had been cleared, an empty downhill road and no waiting passengers gave 1992's motorman the chance to make up for lost time. The car shuddered as it gained speed down St John Street, the wheels screeching as the car took the right-hand curve into Rosebery Avenue. Richard and John felt a sense of exhilaration as 1992 scuttled past grim tenement blocks and then Sadler's Wells theatre before finally slowing down amidst the

warehouses of Clerkenwell Road. As they passed into Theobald's Road, derelict sites and shored-up buildings still bore silent witness to the damage suffered by London in the Blitz, over 10 years earlier. They pulled up at the Bloomsbury stop where a couple of passengers alighted and three more boarded. The conductor rang the bell, hitting it with his ticket rack, and 1992 moved forward, turning left into Southampton Row.

From their front upper-deck seat Richard and John could see looming ahead the cavernous opening of the Kingsway Subway. They sat transfixed as 1992 gained the 1-in-10 slope leading down into the subway, the car then sliding gracefully ever downwards whilst the daylight above faded and then became lost as 1992 entered the blackness of the subway. The sensation of speed increased as 1992 swept along just a few inches clear of the barely-discernible tunnel wall. With its trucks echoing through the tunnel, 1992 suddenly climbed

Below: Former Leyton Corporation 'E/3'-class car No 175 has just entered Clerkenwell Road from Roseberry Avenue to the left. From Islington Green, tram routes 33 and 35 had been paralleled by bus route 19, on which Battersea's RTL482 (KLB 701) is seen. Behind, Wandsworth's RTL1175 (LYF 116) is working route 170, which replaced the greater part of the third Kingsway Subway tram route, 31 (Islington Green–Wandsworth), in Stage 1 of Operation Tramaway, on 1 October 1950. *J. C. Gillham*

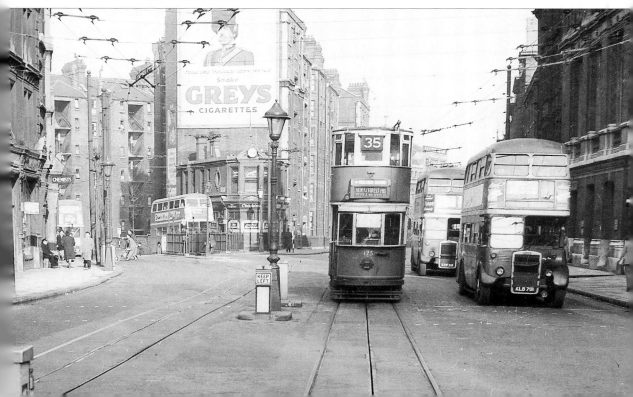

Right: The motorman of 'E/3'-class car No 1998 and Holborn Tramway Station's duty inspector look towards the camera as the southbound car waits at the island platform. As the tram's nearside rear entrance is against the subway wall, passengers would have had to board or alight through the front entrance, beside the motorman. The clock, comprehensive route information and LT roundels, including one set high for upper-deck passengers, lend the scene the *ambience* of a contemporary Underground station — except for the complete lack of advertisements. *V.C.Jones/Ian Allan Library*

Left: The entrance to Aldwych station, in the centre of Kingsway thoroughfare. The subway first opened for passenger traffic on 24 February 1906, using single-deck tramcars. After rebuilding work (started in 1929 to accommodate double-deck trams) had been completed, it was formally reopened on 14 January 1931. *V.C.Jones/Ian Allan Library*

Left: Passenger's-eye view from the front top-deck seat of a tram emerging from the southern portal of the subway onto the Embankment. Rebuilding of Waterloo Bridge in 1937 necessitated a diversion of the subway's exit to this new position, central under the bridge. *C.Carter*

Right: 'E/3'-class car No 1944 waits for the traffic lights (as well as the timekeeper's permission) before emerging onto the Embankment in this 15 March 1952 view. *J.C.Gillham*

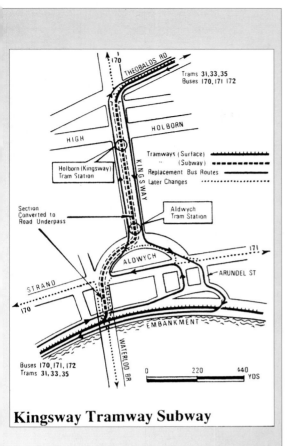

Kingsway Tramway Subway

Map labels:
- 170
- THEOBALDS RD
- Trams 31,33,35 / Buses 170,171,172
- HOLBORN
- HIGH
- Holborn (Kingsway) Tram Station
- Tramways (Surface) / '' (Subway) / Replacement Bus Routes / Later Changes
- KINGSWAY
- Section Converted to Road Underpass
- Aldwych Tram Station
- 171
- ALDWYCH
- ARUNDEL ST
- STRAND
- 170
- EMBANKMENT
- WATERLOO BR
- Buses 170,171,172 / Trams 31,33,35
- 0 220 440 YDS

upwards from a dip, bright lights penetrated the gloom and the car pulled up at Holborn station. An inspector on the platform supervised passengers and 1992 quickly set off again into darkness. Lights ahead growing in intensity, were followed by the silhouette of a tram, travelling on the parallel northbound track, which drew level with 1992; suddenly, with a shuddering movement caused by air turbulence, the two cars passed. Then darkness again, but soon more lights appeared ahead and 1992 slowed down and drew into Aldwych station. Having discharged and picked up passengers, the car set off again, quickly veering to the right under Aldwych and dipping downwards. Richard and John realised that the tram was now in a single-track tunnel as 1992 sped along, the sound of wheels grinding on the continuous curve of the track being but one element of the cacophony of noise. Then the car was back into a twin-track tunnel, a pin-prick of light ahead growing larger and larger until 1992 drew to a halt at traffic lights controlling the southern entrance to the subway underneath Waterloo Bridge. The timekeeper on duty at the entrance spoke quickly to the motorman; then the lights changed and 1992 emerged from the subway and followed tracks which curved right onto Victoria Embankment and joined the tracks of the Embankment routes.

To West Norwood and Forest Hill

With an air of peace and serenity, after the noise of the subway, 1992 progressed along the Embankment past Cleopatra's Needle and underneath Hungerford Bridge. A number of passengers got on or off at Westminster, where Richard and John were afforded an excellent view of the Houses of Parliament. Then 1992 set off again, turning left and then sweeping over Westminster Bridge and past County Hall before heading down Kennington Road. At Kennington Park, route 33 separated from the tracks shared with Woolwich routes 40 and 72 (which went off eastwards towards Camberwell) and was now in splendid isolation as the sole survivor of 11 tram routes which had served Brixton less than two years earlier; 1992 sped along Brixton Road, the motorman seemingly intent on showing that his car could match the speed of the RT-class buses on parallel tram-replacement routes 95 and 109. Richard and John recognised Brixton from their journey there on tram route 78 three months earlier. After clearing Brixton change-pit, 1992 carried on to the West Norwood terminus. Following a quick drink and a pork pie at the nearby 'Thurlow Arms', Richard and John boarded 'E/3'-class car No 1940 and set off at 1.18pm back to the Embankment, the pair leaving 1940 at Westminster just over half an hour later. Watching the transport scene on the bank of the River Thames they could see that Victoria Embankment was an important terminus in London Transport's operations. In a working practice

Above: 'E/3'-class car No 1942 on route 33 and Holloway garage's RT1583 (KLB 671) on route 19 wait for the green light at the western end of Theobald's Road before turning left into Southampton Row and, for the tram, the entrance to the Kingsway Subway. Notice that on the curve the conduit is offset from its more usual central position between the running tracks; this was in order to align it with the radial movement of the trams "ploughs". Behind the news stand on the left lies a still-derelict bomb-site. *C. Carter*

Below: Subway-route motormen were hand-picked men with at least six months' experience on other street routes. They faced their sternest test on the northern uphill ramp out of the subway into Southampton Row, which was controlled by traffic lights, often set against the tram, as shown in this view of 'E/3'-class car No 1948. The motorman would have to hold the car, perhaps by using the first notch of power and no brake; setting off again would often be accompanied by a shower of sparks as steel wheels tried to grip steel track. Sometimes the tram would run backwards, to be jerked to a halt by its embarrassed motorman, using the brakes before trying again. Notching up too quickly could cause the circuit-breakers to blow, isolating power from the motors, and only remedied by resetting the changeover switch. *C. Carter*

Above: The conductor starts to lower the trolley pole of 'E/3'-class car No 1997 (left) while similar car 1992 has just had its pole raised to the overhead wire prior to 'shooting' its plough in this view at Brixton's change-pit in Effra Road, close to its junction with Brixton Hill. The plough-shifter groups spare ploughs for following cars. Beyond the curved conduit slot stands one of the pit's two gas lamps, at the foot of which is a storage box. Nearer the camera is a coke brazier to keep the plough-shifter warm in cold weather. The car passing to the left of 1992 bears both GB and USA plates — perhaps indicative of the pervasive American influence of the period. *C. Carter*

Centre right: Until Stage 1 of Operation Tramaway, the Embankment was served entirely by tram routes, apart from a few Green Line coach services which used the Westminster end; introduced on 1 October 1950, route 168 (Wandsworth–Farringdon Street) was the first bus route to travel the entire length of the Embankment. Southbound journeys used the same section of road as the tram tracks, as demonstrated by Wandsworth garage's RTL1135 (LYF 59) squeezing past 'HR/2'-class car No 1890 at tram route 40's Savoy Street terminus just south of Waterloo Bridge. *C. Carter*

Lower right: 'E/3' class No 1910 was built by Hurst Nelson in 1930. The car is seen on 5 April 1952 literally at the end of the line in Waldram Park Road, Forest Hill — by then the sole remaining South London terminus using the conduit system. Further up the road, another tram waits for No 1910 to clear the terminus's single-line spur for its arrival. *J. C. Gillham*

established by the tramways and still maintained by Abbey Wood tram routes 36 and 38, several tram-replacement bus routes used the Embankment as a gigantic turning loop, with access being gained from Westminster Bridge and departure via Blackfriars Bridge or *vice versa*. Richard and John watched with fascination the continuous stream of activity as the eight bus and six tram routes using the Westminster section of the Embankment gave 144 bus and 104 tramway movements per hour on that Saturday afternoon — about four vehicles every minute.

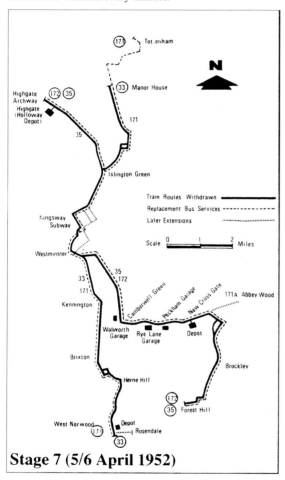

Stage 7 (5/6 April 1952)

Conscious that time pressed, Richard and John boarded conduit-only 'HR/2'-class tram No 118 departing at 2.13pm for Forest Hill on route 35. Parting company with the tracks shared with the Abbey Wood routes 36/38 at Elephant & Castle, the 35 continued down Walworth Road as the sole remaining tram route serving that thoroughfare. At Camberwell Green it joined tracks with Woolwich routes 40 and 72 as far as New Cross; then, after turning south off Lewisham Way, it followed a lengthy one-way working through residential roads to Brockley, before reaching Forest Hill terminus. Absolved from a need to change trolley pole ends, 118 quickly set off northwards, leaving Richard and John at the terminus. They did not find too much other transport interest amidst the suburban domesticity of Forest Hill and, in view of time, debated whether to return direct to Victoria on RTL-operated route 185, which had replaced Blackwall Tunnel tram route 58 on 7 October 1951, or take a last tram ride on route 35 as far as Camberwell Green, from where they could catch a 36 or 36A bus through to Paddington. The arrival of 'E3'-class car 1910, decided matters for them, and, after another quick turnaround, 1910 set off at 3.29pm with the two friends aboard.

A close-run thing

Leaving 1910 amidst the bustle and traffic at Camberwell Green, the pair saw an RT about to set off on the 36. Despite running after it the bus moved off too quickly for them to catch, but they knew that the combined frequency of routes 36 and 36A should give a bus every four minutes. Before long RT3408 appeared with blinds set for a cross-London journey to West Kilburn. After boarding and buying their tickets Richard glanced at his watch, saw that it was 4.10pm and calculated that the bus should just about reach Paddington in time to let them catch the 4.45pm train back to Reading. The friends relaxed as the AEC Regent made good time through Kennington and sped up Vauxhall Bridge Road. This good progress was suddenly halted at Victoria when one of London Transport's omnipresent Inspectors appeared and beckoned to the driver, who opened his cab window, the pair being joined in a conversation over the bonnet by the conductor, who had walked round from the platform.

Operation Tramaway Stage 7 (5/6 April 1952)	
Tram routes withdrawn	**Replacement bus routes**
33 West Norwood–Manor House	171 West Norwood–Tottenham
35 Forest Hill–Highgate Archway	172 Forest Hill–Highgate Archway
35 Bloomsbury–Highgate Archway (All night — Saturday night/ Sunday morning excepted)	292 Charing Cross (LT station)–Highgate Archway (All night — Saturday night/ Sunday morning excepted)

BUSES ON TRAM-REPLACEMENT ROUTES

Above: Work on building Stockwell garage was still incomplete when it became responsible for route 171 on 6 April 1952. In addition to replacing tram route 33 in its entirety, the 171 was extended northwards beyond Manor House to give new bus facilities in the West Green area. RTL1262 (LYR 794), one of Stockwell's initial allocation of 38 RTLs, is seen at the 'Thurlow Arms', West Norwood, shortly after the conversion, when that terminus's single-line spur and overhead tramway wires were still *in situ. C. Carter*

Above: Rye Lane garage's RT2847/9 (LYF 494/6) are seen at New Cross Gate, working route 172 on Last Tram Day — 5 July 1952. The view was taken from the front upper deck of 'E/3'-class car No 1931, which was holding up car 1863 on route 72 until it had used the crossover to follow 1908 on the left. Both 1908 and 1931 had been hired by the Light Railway Transport League for a farewell tour of London tram routes. When photographed, the pair had travelled from Southwark Bridge to New Cross Gate, after which, having executed the crossover manoeuvre, they headed for the Embankment on the next stage of their tour. *W. J. Wyse, courtesy G. W. Morant*

Journey schedule

Saturday 5 April 1952

Terminus	Dep/Arr	Route No	Vehicle	Allocation	Fare
Paddington (Praed Street)	9.12am	Bus 27A	RTL348	R	8d
Highgate (Archway Tavern)	9.40am				
Highgate (Archway LT Station)	10.02am	Tram 35	'HR/2' 132	Highgate	5d
Islington Green	10.17am				
Islington Green	10.44am	Tram 33	'E/3' 1948	Highgate	5d
Manor House (LT Station)	11.02am				
Manor House (LT Station)	11.35am	Tram 33	'E/3' 1992	Norwood	1/-
West Norwood	12.43pm				
West Norwood	1.18pm	Tram 33	'E/3' 1940	Norwood	6d
Embankment (Westminster)	1.52pm				
Embankment (Westminster)	2.13pm	Tram 35	'HR/2' 118	New Cross	9d
Forest Hill	3.03pm				
Forest Hill	3.29pm	Tram 35	'E/3' 1910	New Cross	6d
Camberwell Green	4.00pm				
Camberwell Green	4.08pm	Bus 36	RT3408	PM	} 6d
Victoria (Vauxhall Bridge Rd)	4.27pm				
Victoria (Vauxhall Bridge Rd)	4.28pm	Bus 36A	RTL756	WL	
Paddington Station (Praed Street)	4.43pm				

A minute or so later the conductor re-boarded to tell passengers that RT3408 was being turned short at Victoria and that they should 'Allgetonawonbehinpliz'.

As they joined the other disgruntled passengers on the pavement, Richard told John that such arbitrary practice was quite a common occurrence on London Transport — RT3408 was probably being turned to fill a gap in the southbound service on the route. Anxious for their train connection, they glanced down Vauxhall Bridge Road where before long RTL756 could be seen approaching on route 36A bound for West Kilburn. That bus was already well loaded, but the passengers from RT3408 managed to squeeze aboard. Filled near to capacity, RTL756 headed slowly up Grosvenor Place, around Hyde Park Corner and into Park Lane. Rounding Marble Arch the two friends' hearts sank when they saw a crowd of passengers at the Edgware Road stop, many of whom had been shopping in Oxford Street, judging by their parcels and bags. The seconds ticked away as this throng started to board, until the conductor shouted 'No more room on the bus!' and gave a three-bell ring to indicate a full load to the driver. RTL756 now set off up Edgware Road, gaining speed and leaving intending passengers at other stops to wait for the next bus as it rushed past with its capacity load.

Richard and John, who, displaying the customary good manners of the day, had given up their downstairs seats to two lady passengers, edged towards the platform once the bus had turned into Praed Street. Just short of the station, RTL756 was held up by traffic. Although the practice was officially frowned upon, Richard and John followed the example of countless Londoners and jumped off the platform just as the bus started moving forward again. After a quick glance for other traffic they crossed the street and ran down onto the station concourse. Hastily trying to assimilate information on the departure board, they realised that their train was on Platform 1. Weaving amidst passengers and porters in the station's smoky atmosphere, the pair headed for the rear door of their train, which they scrambled aboard just before the guard waved his green flag.

Richard and John subsequently learnt from their friend Victor Jones that 'E/3'-class car No 185 had worked the last passenger-carrying journey through the Subway in the early hours of Sunday 6 April.

— 4 —

Down the East End and on to Grays

FOR several weeks Richard and John had been contemplating a day's itinerary that would let them savour the unique atmosphere of London's East End whilst also sampling some of the interesting bus and trolleybus operations there. They also wanted to extend their trip to Grays in Essex where the Country Bus Department had recently taken over operation of local Eastern National bus routes. News from a contact in the Southern Counties Touring Society that the last TF-class Green Line coaches on route 720 were about to be replaced by new RF coaches hastened their preparations. They planned a weekday visit on Friday 2 May and, knowing that an early start would be necessary to fit in all objectives, the friends travelled up to London the previous evening. The *Evening News*, which Richard bought for 1½d from a news vendor, carried details of big May Day celebrations held that day in Communist countries.

'Can't ever see May Day becoming a Bank Holiday in this country,' he remarked. John nodded sagely in agreement.

To Aldgate

Next morning they took an early breakfast, settled their hotel bills of 7s 6d each per room with breakfast, left the Cameo Hotel in Vauxhall Bridge Road, glanced quickly at the window display in the nearby Ian Allan bookshop and by 8.30am were at Victoria. The rush hour was well underway as they boarded a heavily-laden City-bound RTW272 on route 11. Travelling past the Bank of England, Richard informed John that nearby Threadneedle Street was one of the narrow central-London

Below: Route 11 (Shepherd's Bush–Liverpool Street) was regarded by LT as its most prestigious service and was often used for official photographs. It was converted to 8ft-wide RTW operation on 11 April 1951, when RTW269 (KXW 369) was among the buses allocated to Riverside garage, which provided 18 of the route's 67-bus Monday-Friday allocation, the remaining 49 coming from Dalston garage. The bus is seen at the wide Charing Cross end of The Strand. *A. B. Cross, courtesy D. A. Ruddom*

ALDGATE MINORIES

Above: Chassisless AEC/Metro-Cammell trolleybus No 1466 (FXH 466) of 1939 formed part of the 150-vehicle 'L3' class — the largest batch of identical trolleybuses to form a continuous delivery to LT. The Poplar-based vehicle is seen on Barking Road route 567, which, combined with routes 565/665, gave a weekday frequency of up to one trolleybus per minute between Aldgate and Barking. This group of interworked routes, which also included route 569, had a Monday-Friday allocation of 118 trolleybuses; this comprised Poplar depot's entire trolleybus allocation, plus others from West Ham.
D. Morris, courtesy T. W. Moore

Left: High-frequency Romford Road Green Line routes 721 (Aldgate–Brentwood) and 722 (Aldgate–Upminster [Corbets Tey]) were double-deck-operated using RT 'coaches' allocated to Romford garage. The routes and garage had been acquired by LT on 10 January 1934 from pioneer operator Edward Hillman's Saloon Coaches Ltd. These vehicles, exemplified by RT3235 (KYY 964), were identical to RT buses except for their Green Line livery, metal LT bullseye motifs (attached to the upper-deck side panels) and the rare (for 1952) concession of saloon heaters.
D. Morris, courtesy T. W. Moore

Right: The TF class was one of the innovative designs which emerged in the 1930s from collaboration between London Transport and manufacturers (in this case Leyland) which sought to dispense with the traditional vertically-mounted front engine; in this instance the Leyland 8.6-litre engine was mounted horizontally in an underfloor position. The LPTB-built body, meanwhile, offered the driver excellent line of sight. TF39 (FJJ 650) waits time on route 720 in front of the LT staff canteen.
J. C. Gillham

Above: Bow depot's 'N1'-class AEC 664T trolleybus No 1627 (FXH 627), bodied by the Birmingham Railway Carriage & Wagon Co, heads south along Whipps Cross Road on route 661 from Lea Bridge to Aldgate. In the background, wartime Nissen huts erected on this southern extremity of Epping Forest have been adapted for residential use, reflecting the chronic housing shortage which still affected the capital. *C. Carter*

thoroughfares along which 8ft-wide RTW-class buses were trialled in 1950 at the insistence of the Metropolitan Police, which was concerned that wider buses might aggravate traffic congestion in Central London. Subsequently, permission had been granted for the use of RTW vehicles on approved routes. Delayed by heavy traffic RTW272 arrived at its stand outside Broad Street station in Liverpool Street four minutes late, at 8.59am. Leaving the bus, the pair walked to nearby Bishopsgate, spending a few minutes there watching terminating trolleybuses on lengthy routes 557 from Chingford and 649 from Waltham Cross turning across the road on what was reputed to be the tightest trolleybus turning circle in London. Moving on, the pair walked down Middlesex Street, imagining the boisterous atmosphere of each Sunday morning's Petticoat Lane Market with its barrow-boys, coster-mongers and crowds of jostling East Enders. After 10 minutes they reached Aldgate High Street and headed towards Minories Coach & Bus Station. Here they marvelled at the fascinating mixture of trolleybuses and Green Line coaches. From a study of timetable displays the pair worked out that 46 trolleybuses and 19 Green Line coaches departed Aldgate every hour in the weekday off-peak period.

South African trolleybuses and some provincial buses

Just after 9.30am TF39 pulled onto the stand for route 720, the crew leaving their vehicle to get a cup of tea in the LT canteen. The two friends boarded the

coach and waited. A few minutes later the refreshed crew reappeared and at 9.47am the driver pressed the starter, springing the horizontally-mounted engine into life. Engaging the preselective gearbox, he eased the Leyland coach out of Aldgate and along Whitechapel Road. The conductor came to collect their fares and was a bit surprised when John told him that they only wanted to go to Leytonstone.

'It'd be cheaper on the 661 trolleybus — you'll each have to pay a shilling minimum fare on Green Line,' he said.

'I know,' John replied, 'but we wanted to ride on one of these TF coaches before they come off Green Line service.'

The conductor smiled as he handed them their Bell-Punch tickets. 'You're only just in time, mate. Our garage at Epping is putting the first RF coaches onto this route tomorrow.'

The 34-seat Leyland passed through Bow to Stratford, where route 720 parted company with double-deck RT-operated Green Line routes 721 and 722 and headed northwards to Leytonstone, where Richard and John left the coach. A local café provided an opportunity for a very welcome cup of coffee, after which the pair headed for the 'Green Man' terminus. SRT115 on route 66 arrived on the stand, where the conductor set the destination blind for Hornchurch. The friends boarded the 1939-built AEC Regent bearing a 1949 Park Royal body and at 10.55am the bus set off through Wanstead and along Eastern Avenue. Although the road was flat and stops were few, the friends became aware that this RT lookalike's performance was sluggish compared with a 'proper' RT-family bus. Having just passed Gants Hill roundabout, they noticed a brown double-deck

Above: In the immediate postwar years LT found that body supply was outstripping delivery of new RT chassis. The SRT class was created following a decision to modify the chassis of 300 prewar STL-class AEC Regents to take standard RT-style bodies. Unfortunately, operational experience soon revealed that the extra body weight was excessive for the engine's capacity, resulting in poor performance. The order for SRTs was cut back to 160 vehicles, and by deliberate policy they were generally allocated to less onerous outer-London routes such as the 66 (Leytonstone–Hornchurch), upon which 1949-built SRT147 (DLU 24) — the chassis of which originated with STL2041 of 1937 — is seen in Eastern Avenue. *A.B.Cross*

Left: The former City Coach Co 15min-frequency route from Wood Green to Southend-on-Sea was one of three long-distance, limited-stop bus routes allowed to carry passengers within the LT area, albeit at premium fares; the others were Birch Bros route 203 to Rushden and Thames Valley route B to Reading. These escaped compulsory acquisition under the 1933 Act because their outer termini were well beyond the limit of LT's operational authority. Joint operation — an apparent anathema to LT in any case — could not be pursued, as the outer termini were well beyond the 10-mile (5-mile in Kent) extension beyond the London Passenger Transport Area within which LT was permitted to undertake such activities; the alternative, of splitting these routes at or near the LPTA boundary, would have negated their usefulness. By 1952 all were double-deck-operated. City's fleet, which passed to BTC-controlled Westcliff-on-Sea Motor Services on 17 February, included 1949 Beadle-bodied Leyland Titan PD1A No LD16 (NVX 313), seen passing along Eastern Avenue at Newbury Park station. *W.J.Wyse, courtesy G.W.Morant*

Above: The 'SA'-class 'South African' trolleybuses were built to the order of the Durban and Johannesburg undertakings. Due to the threats posed by German U-boats to Allied merchant shipping in World War 2, only essential convoys were despatched. Thus between 1941 and 1943 these non-standard trolleybuses became the first 8ft-wide vehicles in LT's fleet, with the front exit doors specified by their originally-intended operators blanked off. They also featured non-standard extra-wide, one-piece front destination apertures, and, perhaps uniquely for LT, the blind-makers had to stitch together separate number and destination blinds to make up a complete display. 'SA2'-class Metro-Cammell-bodied Leyland TTB No 1735 (GLB 735) passes the Horns Tavern in narrow Horns Road, Ilford. The successful operation of these 8ft-wide vehicles did much to overcome official prejudice, paving the way for the introduction of the RTW class. *C. Carter*

Leyland Titan PD1 pull up behind them. They realised that this was one of the former City Coach Company buses now in the ownership of Tilling company Westcliff-on-Sea, following City's sale to the BTC on 17 February 1952. The Southend-bound Leyland overtook and pulled away from the SRT down Eastern Avenue towards Newbury Park.

Richard and John were keen to see the South African 'SA'-class trolleybuses about which they had heard so much. Knowing that all this class were based at Ilford trolleybus depot for use on routes 691, 693 and 695, they left the SRT at Newbury Park. Trolleybus wires crossing Eastern Avenue from Horns Road to the north showed where route 691 emerged. They spent a while watching the frequent appearance of trolleybuses on this 3min-frequency route before walking south down Ley Street to see Ilford trolleybus depot.

Time pressed inexorably onwards. By midday Richard and John had walked back to Newbury Park station, where one minute later they boarded SRT154 to continue their journey along Eastern Avenue on route 66. Approaching Romford along North Street, they noticed that the sign in front of a large building under construction proclaimed that this would be the site of LT's new North Street bus garage due to open in 1953. Leaving the SRT at Romford Market, the pair were in need of further refreshment, which was found in a nearby Milk Bar. Suitably fortified, they had time for a quick glance at bus operations in Romford. London Transport provided a good variety of vehicle types in the town, but, uniquely in the Central Area, other operators' routes were quite plentiful too. Former City Daimler CVD6 and Leyland Titan PD1 double-deckers now with Westcliff-on-Sea for the 15min-frequency Wood Green–Southend-on-Sea route mingled with that same operator's Bristol K5G double-deckers working into Romford on route 2A, also from Southend. Bristol K5Gs were in evidence too on Eastern National's lengthy 30min-frequency route 10, which passed through Romford *en route* from Chelmsford to Bow.

SOON TO DISAPPEAR: VARIETY IN ROMFORD

Left: Lengthy route 175 (Poplar–Stapleford Abbots) had a 62-bus Monday-Friday allocation, which by May 1952 was at an advanced stage of conversion to RT- and RTL-class double-deckers. Upton Park garage's 1945 Northern Counties-bodied Guy Arab II G290 (GYL 430) makes a (by now) rare appearance in South Street, Romford, probably on a cross-working allocation with route 101, heading for Poplar terminus, displayed on the destination blind as 'Blackwall Tunnel'. This bus was withdrawn from service in July 1952 and subsequently passed to Western SMT.
A.B.Cross, courtesy D.A.Ruddom

Above: Hornchurch garage's 1937-built STL1696 (DGX 215) is seen at the same spot on a short working to Dagenham New Road. Roof-mounted front route-number boxes (in this instance blanked off) were introduced in 1936 to enhance the appearance of advertisements on the front panels.
A.B.Cross, courtesy D.A.Ruddom

Left: The conductor of STL948 (CGJ 40) is wearing his summer dustcoat as he chats to his driver on the stand outside Romford station. The 247, with a 30min frequency, could almost have been a Country Area route, serving as it did rural communities at Tyler's Cross and Warley on its way to the market town of Brentwood.
A.B.Cross, courtesy D.A.Ruddom

Country Bus at Grays

Regretting that they had but limited time to spend in Romford, the pair boarded RT4123 on route 370 to Grays and Tilbury Ferry. This route formed part of LT's Country Bus operation in South Essex, isolated from physical connection with other parts of the Country Bus network. Setting off at 12.57pm, the RT soon passed Hornchurch garage, whose inadequate capacity necessitated some buses' being parked out overnight in nearby streets. At Upminster the AEC Regent headed southwards, leaving the Central Area at Corbets Tey and pressing on into a landscape pitted with working quarries and pits. Distant chimneys of several cement works grew larger in size as the bus approached the busy little town of Grays.

Richard and John knew that the British Transport Commission, following its acquisition of the Tilling Group in November 1948, had sought to rationalise operations between constituent undertakings in various parts of the country. London Transport, ultimately controlled by the BTC, had been drawn into one such scheme, which resulted in the transfer of Eastern National's local bus operations in the Grays/Tilbury area to London Transport on 30 September 1951. On that date 13 local bus routes, the company's garage in Argent Street, Grays, and 200 staff became the responsibility of London Transport. LT continued to work the EN routes unchanged for three months, supplementing loaned Eastern National buses with increasing numbers of its own STL- and (later) RT-class double-deckers. The main stage of the scheme was

implemented on 2 January 1952, when a completely revised route network was introduced. The former EN garage was closed for operational purposes, as all buses now worked from LT's garage in Hogg Lane, its outside parking area having been considerably extended to cope with the increased number of vehicles.

The pair spent over an hour in Grays viewing bus operations in this extended but isolated outpost of the Country Bus Department. Just after 3pm they made their way to the War Memorial terminal, where Green Line coach RF222 pulled up on route 723A bound for Aldgate. Richard and John boarded their second underfloor-engined coach of the day, setting off at 3.08pm. The familiar, smooth tone of the AEC engine was audible as the driver progressed up through the preselector gearbox. Passing through Aveley LCC housing estate, they noticed that the conductor was responsible for working the front power-operated doors, although the driver sat beside them and generally had a much clearer view. Joining the westbound A13 road at Aveley, the route now ran parallel to the Thames Estuary, past expanses of flat, tree-less fields bordering mud flats alongside the river.

Red LT buses at Rainham indicated that the coach had re-entered the Central Area, and, as it pressed on westwards, the exposed estuary landscape changed from pastoral to industrial. Factories and warehouses, tips and dumps covered the land towards the river, whilst on the landward side of the A13 vast council housing estates stretched into the far distance. The Ford Motor

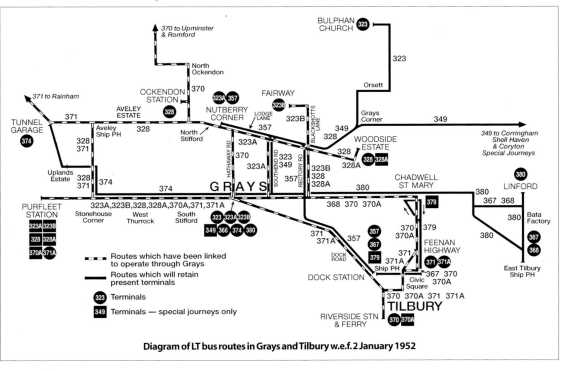

Diagram of LT bus routes in Grays and Tilbury w.e.f. 2 January 1952

GRAYS

Left: Short route 323B to Fairway had been one of two Grays town services previously operated jointly by Eastern National and Grays' (then) sole remaining independent bus operator, Our Bus Service.
The latter sold out to Eastern National on 15 September 1951 as a prelude to the main transfer of Eastern National's Grays routes to London Transport on 30 September.
Seen on layover in Grays, 56-seat Weymann-bodied RT4194 (LYF 253) makes the contrast in both style and capacity with the 20-seat Guy Vixen saloon used previously by Our Bus Service. *A.B.Cross*

Right: STL2170 (DYL 822) had just worked into Grays on route 368 whose use was restricted to employees of the BATA shoe factory at East Tilbury.
Acquisition of this and similar routes 349 and 367 from Eastern National introduced five-day workman's tickets to the LT system. *A.B.Cross*

Co's massive works at Dagenham, served by four LT bus routes, provided an awesome spectacle.

At Rippleside roundabout the Green Line forked right off the A13 along Ripple Road into Barking. Now passing beneath LT trolleybus wires, the coach headed along Barking Road to be held up behind 'L3'-class trolleybus No 1529 working route 665, which had stopped to pick up a crowd of school children. Bound for Bloomsbury, an hour's journey-time away, 1529 set off followed by RF222, which was prevented from overtaking the trolleybus, even at stops, by heavy oncoming traffic. The convoy slowly trailed into East Ham where Richard and John alighted at 3.55pm.

Round the Docks

Richard and John spent about 45 minutes watching activities in East Ham High Street before boarding utility Northern Counties-bodied Guy Arab II G304 bound for North Woolwich. The bus started off, the unmistakable throb of a Gardner five-cylinder engine making conversation difficult as the Guy shuddered down the High Street and across the East Ham/Barking by-pass. The conductor collected their fares, having to ask them to repeat their destination as he had difficulty hearing above the cacophony of sounds inside the bus. As they passed down isolated East Ham Manor Way, the scene ahead from their front upper-deck seat became almost surreal: to the left of the bus, tall chimneys at

Beckton Gas Works belched thick plumes of black smoke into the sky; ahead, giant ships, which dwarfed the landscape, seemed to be rooted into the ground, surrounded by cranes and jibs.

'Anyone for Cyprus?' shouted the conductor, completing the sense of unreality, as Richard and John looked at each other, unable to reconcile the name of the exotic Mediterranean island with the small clutch of Victorian terraced houses that the bus had just pulled up alongside. To their further surprise, one of LT's ubiquitous inspectors was waiting here. In a quick conversation with the bus crew he was heard to inform them that the swing bridge across the entrance to Royal Albert Dock — that explained the ships — was due to be opened shortly but that their bus should get across

before this if it set off quickly; he would turn following buses short at Cyprus. In his haste to get moving the driver crashed the gears before G304 moved away. But too late. Ahead they could see the swing bridge starting to open, and the Guy was forced to pull up and stop at the controlling traffic lights. The driver and conductor conferred, briefly discussing the idea of turning back to Cyprus, but, aware of the 45 or so passengers on board that included dock workers heading for a late shift at the further distant King George V Dock, decided to stay put, and the driver switched off the Gardner engine.

In the sudden silence, Richard and John heard the conductor explain: 'Probably be here a blinking half hour.' Passengers and crew watched as a large cargo ship eased from her berth at the Royal Albert Dock, then

LAST STRONGHOLD OF LONDON'S UTILITY GUY ARABS

As 1952 progressed, Upton Park garage's utility Guy Arab IIs working route 101 (North Woolwich–Wanstead, with Summer Sunday extension to Lambourne End) became the last examples to remain in passenger-carrying service. The survivors were finally taken out of service after operation on 24 December 1952. LT's intake of 435 utility Guy Arab Is and IIs had between them carried six makes of bodywork. The three varieties which remained in service towards the end are illustrated here — all mounted on the Arab II chassis, distinguishable by the forward-projecting radiator 'snout' to allow the optional fitting of a Gardner 6LW engine, although LT's were all fitted with the smaller-capacity 5LW version. The following three photographs were all taken in East Ham High Street South.

Top: Northern Counties bodies were the most handsome of the various utility styles, featuring a curved rear dome as exemplified by G309 (GYL 449). These bodies were of metal-framed construction, which contributed to their longevity. *J.C.Gillham*

Centre: G425 (HGC 204) carried Weymann bodywork which incorporated a slight curvature to the rear dome. *J.C.Gillham*

Bottom: G432 (HGC 211) displays its very angular Park Royal bodywork. *J.C.Gillham*

Above: West Ham depot's 'L3'-class chassisless AEC/Metro-Cammell trolleybus No 1398 (FXH 398) unloads at North Woolwich. This area was administered by the Borough of Woolwich on the south side of the River Thames, leading to the anomaly of 'Kent in Essex'. Part of the berth of the Woolwich Free Ferry, operated by London County Council for the conveyance of vehicles and pedestrians across the Thames, is visible to the right of the picture. Pedestrians could also choose to use a foot tunnel underneath the Thames, built in 1912. The staircase entrance to this is contained in the round tower towards the left of the picture. *C. Carter*

slowly headed through the narrow neck of water past G304 at the dock gate, beyond which lay the River Thames. With the ship's manœuvre completed, the swing bridge moved back into position, and, after a delay of 20 minutes, G304's engine sprang into life and the bus moved off again, traversing without delay another swing bridge at King George V Dock, then throbbing along a twisty run to reach North Woolwich at 5.19pm. At the end of a working day this was a very busy spot. Paddle-steamers of the Woolwich Free Ferry crossed the River Thames every few minutes, embarking and disembarking passengers to and from Woolwich. These included many dock workers arriving at North Woolwich on trolleybus routes 569, 669 and 685, as well as bus route 101.

After a while Richard and John walked towards Silvertown. Knowing that they had to return home to Reading that evening, they boarded 'L3'-class trolleybus No 1487 outside Silvertown station at 6.15pm. No 1487 was working that day's last evening peak-hour journey on route 569 to Aldgate. The 12-year-old chassisless AEC went along Silvertown Way, a brand-new road to the docks opened in 1934, then traversed East India

Dock Road, passing through Canning Town, Poplar and Limehouse.

Along Commercial Road in Stepney a middle-aged couple in most extraordinary and eye-catching clothes boarded the trolleybus and occupied the pair of seats immediately in front of Richard and John. The friends looked at each other.

'I think they're a Pearly King and Queen', ventured John.

'That's right, mate,' said the man, turning round with a smile. 'We're off to a charity "do" down Whitechapel for Barnardo's. Always use the Last Resort.'

'What do you mean, "Last Resort"?' asked John.

'Cockney rhyming slang, mate. "Last Resort" means London Transport,' replied the Pearly King. He paused for a few seconds before adding, with a genuine sense of pride, 'Best transport set-up in the country and no mistake.'

Those last words echoed in their minds for the rest of their journey from Aldgate to Victoria on route 10 and thence home to Reading by Thames Valley coach. Yes, they agreed, London Transport was indeed the best transport set-up in the country . . . if not the world.

Above: The workaday world of East London is encapsulated in this view at Silvertown dominated by the massive Tate & Lyle sugar refinery separated from the roadway by the North Woolwich railway. West Ham depot's 1938-built 'E2C'-class AEC 664T trolleybus rebodied by Northern Coachbuilders in 1946 following wartime damage No 623C (DLY 623) has just completed a terminus working circuit around the streets of terraced houses to the left; it is now heading along cobbled Albert Road for the stop at Silvertown station, where it will take up a journey on route 685 to Walthamstow 'Crooked Billet'. *C. Carter*

Below: The funnel of a ship in the Royal Albert Dock is visible as two 1937-built trolleybuses meet up on the eastern side of the Silvertown by-pass. Heading away from the camera is 590 (DLY 590), a Brush-bodied AEC 664T passing 638 (DLY 638) a similar Park Royal-bodied model. *C. Carter*

Above: 'E/1'-class Brush-bodied AEC 664T trolleybus No 601 (DLY 601) of 1937 heads up Silvertown Way on route 685, leading another trolleybus on route 669. Cranes rising above Victoria Dock are visible to the left, whilst the Tate & Lyle sugar refinery dominates the distant background to the right. *C. Carter*

Journey schedule

Friday 2 May 1952

Terminus	Dep/Arr	Route No	Vehicle	Garage Allocation	Fare
Victoria (Clock Tower) Liverpool Street Stn	8.33am 8.59am	11	RTW272	R	6d
Aldgate (Minories) Leytonstone (Thatched House)	9.43am 10.03am	720	TF39	EP	1/-
Leytonstone (Green Man) Newbury Park Station	10.55am 11.11am	66	SRT115	G	5d
Newbury Park Station Romford Market	12.01pm 12.23pm	66	SRT154	G	6d
Romford Station Grays (Queen's Hotel)	12.57pm 1.44pm	370	RT4123	GY	1/3d
Grays (War Memorial) East Ham Town Hall	3.08pm 3.55pm	723A	RF222	GY	1/11d
East Ham Town Hall North Woolwich (Free Ferry)	4.46pm 5.19pm	101	G304	U	5d
Silvertown Station Aldgate Minories	6.15pm 6.50pm	569	'L3'1487	PR	8d
Aldgate Station Victoria (Station Forecourt)	7.04pm 7.32pm	10	RT1500	GM	6d

Above: Towards the end of June most surviving serviceable London trams appeared displaying in their side advertising panels a white banner bearing the red wording: 'LAST TRAM WEEK. ON JULY 5 WE SAY GOODBYE TO LONDON'. Exceptions were the ex-West Ham cars, whose shallower panels could not accommodate the banner. Queen Boadicea in her chariot bids a symbolic farewell to 'E/3'-class car No 1922 as it leaves Victoria Embankment to head over Westminster Bridge. The motorman has his left hand on the controller whilst his right hand may be seen resting on the handbrake. The Metropolitan Police licence plate for the tram, 1634 (quite separate from the fleet number), which had to be displayed at one end may clearly be seen on the offside entrance, across which a chain and raised steps prevent any passengers from attempting to board or alight on the 'wrong' side whilst the tram is working in this direction. *Aviation & Transport Photographs, courtesy R. Marshall*

Below: An RT bus passing over Waterloo Bridge symbolises the motorbus's ascendancy over the tram on the Embankment, below. 'E/3'-class car No 1953 has just passed underneath the bridge beside the now-closed southern portal of the Kingsway Subway. *C. Carter*

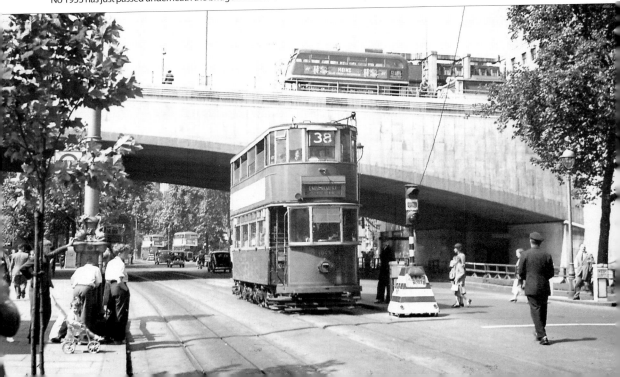

5

A Long Day's Night

'WE'LL see history being made,' said Richard to John as they travelled on Thames Valley's first departure of the day from Reading to London on Saturday 5 July. The two friends had planned by far their most ambitious itinerary yet, which would let them travel over all London's remaining tram networks on this final day of operation, see the actual last trams and, by sacrificing a night's sleep, sample some of the replacement bus routes the next day. Emerging from Victoria Coach Station at 9.10am on a bright sunny morning, they felt buoyed-up by the fine weather as they walked briskly down Victoria Street, past Westminster Abbey and the Houses of Parliament — which, even at that early hour, had attracted some American tourists — to the Embankment.

The Embankment loop

After quickly drinking cups of tea bought at a kiosk they boarded 'E/3'-class tram No 1923 on route 36 just as Big Ben chimed 10 o'clock. Richard found two 3d bits in his change to buy their tickets, and just eight minutes later they left No 1923 at the busy Elephant & Castle. That day only trams on Abbey Wood routes 36 and 38 echoed across this busy interchange where once 19 tram routes had met. The ascendant bus now dominated this junction, served by 27 day and three night bus routes, plus five Green Line services, scheduled to give 605 bus/coach movements at this spot at Monday-Friday peak times, making 'the Elephant' London's most intensely-bussed point outside the centre of London.

Richard and John risked the traffic, crossing to a northbound tram route 36 stop; they wanted to take this final opportunity to travel round the Embankment terminal loop by tram. 'E/3' car No 1948 arrived on route 36, and they boarded, noting that this car had been transferred from Highgate to New Cross depot after the abandonment of the Kingsway Subway services in April. The car set off up London Road, crossing St George's Circus into Blackfriars Road and then across Blackfriars Bridge, after which it turned left down the Victoria Embankment. Now travelling parallel to the River Thames, the pair saw buses emerging onto the Embankment from Temple Place, following the indirect route which buses had to follow after replacing tram routes through the Kingsway Subway.

Passing beneath Waterloo Bridge, route 36 reached its terminus at Savoy Street, just south of the bridge, where the remaining passengers alighted, but Richard and John stayed put. They noticed a considerable crowd waiting at the tram stop and a goodly number of new passengers boarded. After a couple of minutes they heard the bell ring, and 1948 set off to complete its circuit of the Embankment, leaving via Westminster Bridge. This time they stayed on the tram past Elephant

Above: One of London's more obscure occupations disappeared with the trams. Pointsmen were stationed at busy tramway junctions to operate a points lever to minimise disruption to schedules. This gentleman, seen in his hut at Bricklayer's Arms (which afforded some protection against bad weather), survived until the end of the trams. Latterly he had only to operate the points for trams heading along the Old Kent Road bound for either New Kent Road (routes 36/38) or Great Dover Street (route 46); a year earlier he would have been much busier, with six daytime tram routes to watch out for. *J.C.Gillham*

Above: 'E/3'-class car No 1931 stands as Southwark Bridge on route 46, the last survivor of six tram routes which once served this terminus. No 1931, chosen for the co-incidence of its fleetnumber with the year, had the distinction of being the official tram at the re-opening ceremony of the Kingsway Subway for double-deck operation on 14 January 1931, for which a special white livery was applied. *C. Carter*

Below: Caught by the camera on one of the last occasions on which the crossover in New Cross Gate would be used, the conductor of 'E/3' class No 1926 pulls a point-iron to let his car gain the adjacent track in order to return to Kennington on 5 July 1952. Peckham garage's brand-new RT2917 (MLL 664) approaches on route 36. *W. J. Wyse, courtesy G. W. Morant*

& Castle to alight in the Old Kent Road at Bricklayers Arms — one of the London's oldest hostelries, dating back to 1346. Wishing to take this last day's opportunity to ride on a tram to Southwark Bridge, they crossed into Great Dover Street and at 11.09am boarded ex-West Ham car No 341 for the 5min journey to the Southwark terminus. Recalling their visit there six months earlier, on the last day of tram routes 48 to West Norwood and 52 to Grove Park, they headed for the kiosk near Cannon Street station for some refreshment.

To Woolwich and Abbey Wood

On their return to Southwark Bridge, Richard and John were greeted by the sight of tram No 83, an 'E/1'-class survivor once in the East Ham fleet. Boarding and obtaining their favourite top-deck front seat, the pair settled down for an hour's tram ride on route 46. No 83 set off at 11.42am, the first 30 minutes of the journey through New Cross and down to Lewisham being familiar from their journey on tram route 52 six months earlier. From Lewisham the car headed along Lee High Road before reaching the change-pit by Leyland Avenue in Lee Green. Here the conductor raised the trolley pole to the overhead wires and the pit shifter removed the plough, after which 83 continued under overhead power into affluent suburbia past large houses set in leafy

avenues. A few minutes later, Richard and John saw ahead of them a large roundabout at Eltham Green. Stopping to pick up passengers in Eltham Road, 83 moved off and negotiated this complex as it turned up Eltham Hill. Leaving Eltham with a good passenger load, the 'E/1' now headed due north. Just before the junction with the A2 Rochester Way, metals from Westhorne Avenue used by route 72 joined those from Eltham. Crossing Shooters Hill, 83 then passed the magnificent façade of the Royal Military Academy before heading downhill along Grand Depot Road into Woolwich.

Richard and John left 83 at Beresford Square terminus and were rather amazed to see trams edging their way through crowds of shoppers at the market stalls. A clock struck 1 o'clock just as a siren sounded, and hordes of workers emerged from Woolwich Arsenal to head for home on trams or buses. Richard and John squeezed onto 'E/1'-class tram No 592 working route 38 to Abbey Wood. The tram eased its way out of Woolwich along Plumstead Road, taking power from the positive wire of the trolleybus overhead used by routes 696/698. The road narrowed as 592 worked along Plumstead High Street, whilst, ahead, Richard and John could see the two tram tracks merge into single-line working. Progress through Plumstead was slow as 592 negotiated no fewer than five stretches of single-track working, sometimes having to give

Below: The hazards presented to other road users by the trams' *modus operandi* cannot be denied in this view at Lewisham. Crowds, no doubt swelled by those wishing to take a last tram ride, block the roadway on 5 July 1952 as No 83 stops to load. On the opposite side, Sidcup's RTL188 (KGK 852) works route 21, which would be strengthened from the following day in partial replacement of tram route 46. *W. J. Wyse, courtesy G. W. Morant*

Above: Many East Kent and Maidstone & District express services shared their southeasterly approach to London with tram routes through Eltham, Lewisham and New Cross. On 5 July 1952 East Kent 1935 Park Royal-bodied Leyland Tiger TS7 coach JG 5434, converted from petrol to diesel engine only the previous year, runs beside 'HR/2'-class car No 1863 just west of Lee Green. *W. J. Wyse, courtesy G. W. Morant*

Left: The section of tram track between Lee Green change-pit (to the east of Lee Green) and Lee Green itself was equipped for both conduit and overhead-power operation. This was done to avoid the irksome chore (for tramcars on short workings from Woolwich to Lee Green) of having to take up a 'plough' for the final few hundred yards of their journey and then having to 'shoot' it again on returning a few minutes later in the Woolwich direction. The conductor of No 83 raises the car's trolley pole in Lee Green, although his driver will not be able to switch over from conduit power to overhead until the car has shot its 'plough' at the change-pit further on. Again, hazards to alighting passengers and other road users are readily apparent in this view.
W. J. Wyse, courtesy G. W. Morant

Right: Something has gone awry at Eltham Green roundabout. The conductor of an 'HR/2'-class car on route 72, heading up Westhorne Avenue on the direct route to Woolwich, struggles to get his car's dislodged trolley pole back onto the overhead wire, assisted by a mechanic, which suggests that a repetitive problem had developed. The approach to this junction was controlled by overhead points, in which the 'frog' would be tripped in a particular direction if the car took power at the point or would remain static if the car coasted past not under power. Former East Ham car 92 on route 46 avoids any difficulty, since its routing takes it the 'long' way, both around the roundabout and to Woolwich via Eltham. *D. W. K. Jones, courtesy J. C. Gillham*

precedence to oncoming cars. Eventually back on double track, Richard and John noticed that the overhead power supply for the tram was now separate from that for trolleybuses. No 592 turned left off Bostall Hill into an area of neat suburban houses; still paralleled by trolleybus route 698, the tram headed along McLeod Road, their upper-deck seat affording Richard and John glimpses of flat marshland leading down to the Thames Estuary, visible behind the ranks of red-bricked semi-detached houses. They could see excavation and building work underway on this vast desolate expanse of land; John told Richard that he had read that London County Council was developing a large housing estate there, to be called the 'Abbey Estate'. After taking a

Below: In Woolwich, trams performed a one-way circuit around the town centre, part of which led them through the crowded Market. Former West Ham car No 312 pauses there on Last Tram Day before working to Middle Park Avenue on route 44, itself effectively a short working of the 46. *C. Carter*

Above: 'E/3'-class car No 183 passes along McLeod Road, Abbey Wood on Last Tram Day. On the right may be seen examples of the prefabricated houses — 'prefabs' — which evolved from the need for cheap, speedily-erected accommodation to deal with the chronic housing shortages following World War 2. *A. D. Packer*

Below: 'E/3'-class tramcar No 184 and 'H1'-class Metro-Cammell-bodied Leyland trolleybus No 805 (ELB 805), using separate overhead wires, are seen side by side in McLeod Road, Abbey Wood, on Last Tram Day. *A. D. Packer*

Right: 'E/3' car No 184 has now turned the corner from McLeod Road into Knee Hill, approaching the Abbey Wood terminus on 5 July 1952. *A.D. Packer*

sharp left turn into Knee Hill, 592 coasted downhill towards the Abbey Wood terminus.

The weather that day had produced a real scorcher! Feeling extremely thirsty now after over three hours of more-or-less continuous tram travel, Richard and John entered the Harrow Inn adjacent to the terminus. Here, cold pints of shandy slaked their thirst as they tried the dish of whelks with bread recommended by the landlord. 'Londoners love shellfish!' he exclaimed. 'Caught fresh today here in Kent.'

Suitably fortified, they left the Harrow Inn at 2 o'clock and went to look at Abbey Wood tram depot, around the corner in Abbey Wood Road. Returning towards the tram terminus, they broke into a run as they saw an 'E/3' car about to set off on route 38, but it glided slowly up the hill and away from them. 'No problem really,' said Richard. 'The next one will be in about three minutes.' At that moment 'E/3'-class car No 1923, bearing a stencil for route 36, moved to complete a crossover onto the 'up' track. Sweating somewhat from their exertion on this hot day, they waited until 1923 had completed its manœuvre, and boarded. At 2.14pm the conductor characteristically hit the bell-press with his ticket rack and the car set off.

Below: Abbey Wood tram depot remained operational while the site was rebuilt for motor-bus use. Former East Ham car No 91 stands by the entrance. *C. Carter*

Eltham routes

Buying 3d tickets to Woolwich, the pair retraced their earlier journey through Plumstead to Beresford Square, where they alighted at 2.29pm. The day had become seriously warm by now, with temperatures around 80°F. Still thirsty, Richard and John bought 3d bottles of Tizer from a stall in the market, after which, drinking from the bottles, they watched the crowds using the trams. Although a Saturday afternoon was always busy with shoppers, it became clear that many more Londoners had turned out simply to take this last chance to ride on their once-familiar form of street transport destined to pass into the history books the next day. Queues much longer than normal formed at the tram stops as departing trams set off full to capacity yet still leaving many intending passengers waiting. The tram system was being overwhelmed by demand on its final day.

Above: Although it was separated by an ocean in terms of both distance and culture from Tennessee Williams' Deep South, someone had tried to transform South London 'E/1'-class tram No 593 into A Streetcar Named 'Desire'. Young and not-so-young passengers store up memories on Last Tram Day. *W. J. Wyse, courtesy G. W. Morant*

Richard and John wanted to travel on every remaining section of route, so just after 3 o'clock joined the tram queue in Beresford Square. Shoulder to shoulder, they shuffled slowly forwards towards the head of the queue as each tram departed fully-laden. 'HR/2'-class car No 1859 came into view on route 72 to Embankment. They squeezed aboard, going upstairs and getting seats halfway down the car. At 3.13pm 1859 set off, completing the one-way circuit in Woolwich before heading up Woolwich New Road. Route 72 retraced their earlier journey into Woolwich by route 46 as far as the junction with the A2 at Rochester Way. Here the tracks for route 72 branched off to the right down Westhorne Avenue, thereby affording route 72 a direct link to Eltham Green, avoiding the 'dog's leg' through Eltham used by routes 44 and 46. Car 1859 negotiated the roundabout complex at Eltham Green before stopping in Eltham Road at Middle Park Avenue terminus, where Richard and John alighted. They spent the next 45 minutes watching operations at Eltham

Left: 'E/3'-class car No 1931, hired by the Light Railway Transport League, has its trolley pole lowered after taking up the 'plough' for the very last time at Woolwich change-pit at 6.30pm on Last Tram Day. A chalked-on fleetname has restored the tram's ownership to London County Council Tramways! In all, six 'E/3s' were hired for private charter on Last Tram Day: Nos 1908 and 1931 by the Light Railway Transport League, 1898 and 1909 by the Ian Allan Bus Spotters' Club, 1946 by The Omnibus Society and 1988 by the Infantile Paralysis Fellowship of London. *W. J. Wyse, courtesy G. W. Morant*

TWILIGHT OF THE TRAMS AT ELTHAM GREEN ROUNDABOUT

By afternoon on Last Tram Day, many tramcars had gained chalked slogans and other remarks on their bodywork.
Souvenir-hunters were at work too, as route sideboards, route-number stencils and even destination blinds started to disappear.

Above: 'HR/2'-class car No 1862 has already lost its route sideboard as it scuttles past on the north side of the roundabout. *J.C.Gillham*

Above: Former East Ham 'E/1'-class car No 87 is seen on the roundabout's eastern side, about to follow the left-hand track up Eltham Hill. An apocryphal account credits this car with making the last passenger-carrying journey on the London Transport system. Reputedly its arrival at Woolwich Beresford Square on the last route 46 working was delayed from a scheduled 12.17am on Sunday 6 July 1952 to 1.55am, due to hold-ups *en route. W.J.Wyse, courtesy G.W.Morant*

Right: Unique former LCC car No 2, rebuilt to a modern style in 1933, continued in service until the last day. Here, with 'standing room only', it passes the 'Yorkshire Grey' pub on the western side of the roundabout. *J.C.Gillham*

Green, each tramcar that passed being loaded close to capacity with tram enthusiasts and the general public. At 4.17pm Richard and John boarded ex-West Ham car No 307 working route 44 — effectively a short working of route 46 between Middle Park Avenue and Woolwich — and returned to Beresford Square, which they reached about 20 minutes later.

Richard and John spent the next two hours or so in Woolwich. After 5 o'clock the shopping crowds thinned, but greater-than-usual numbers of passengers were still using the trams. Walking down to Woolwich change-pit nearby in Market Hill (close to the Free Ferry), Richard and John spent a while watching the 'plough-shifter' performing his unique duties for the last time. The nearby Vermont Café — at the time, American themes were much in vogue, giving an illusion of prosperity in a still austerity-hit Britain — provided welcome respite from the hot and dusty street. With their energy renewed after mugs of sweet tea and plates of beans on toast, the pair re-emerged to notice that a goodly number of transport enthusiasts were about. As they chatted, the two 'E/3'-class cars hired by the Light Railway Transport League for its farewell tour arrived at Woolwich change-pit. Lingering with the crowd, Richard felt a tap on his shoulder and turned round to see that Prince Marshall, the manager of the Ian Allan bookshop, had remembered him from his and John's visit six months earlier, on the occasion of the end of trams at Victoria. Eagerly they discussed their experiences of the day and plans for the evening, agreeing to meet up later that night at New Cross depot, where the last service trams would terminate.

Back to Town

Richard and John still had to travel the remaining tracks through Greenwich, so at 6.50pm they boarded tram No 168 — an 'E/3' class originally owned by Leyton Corporation — working route 40 to the Embankment. The well-loaded car set off out of Woolwich, a few minutes later passing the Penhall Road 'Tramatorium'. A group of enthusiasts stood around the gate leading to this mournful yard where stood row after row of redundant tramcars whose wheels would turn no more. A little further along, 168 passed Charlton Works, now having overhauled its last tram, and destined to carry on in the future as one of London's two principal trolleybus repair shops. No 168 then entered ancient Greenwich, passing the Royal Naval College buildings. Leaving Greenwich the car headed for New Cross where route 40 met up with the tracks of Woolwich routes 46 and 72 from Eltham. The route from New Cross to Kennington and Camberwell replicated Richard's and John's journey six months earlier on route 54 from Grove Park. At Kennington Park tram routes 40 and 72 headed northwards up Kennington Road, over Westminster Bridge and along the Embankment to terminate at Savoy Street, where Richard and John left 168 at 7.53pm.

Feeling tired from the day's extensive travel and debilitated by the heat, both knew that they needed some time off their feet as well as a decent meal if they were to continue with their plans to see the last trams later that night. Making their way across the Strand,

Above: Unusual sections of tram track continued in use right to the end. 'This section of single track in Greenwich High Road carried conduit slots for tramcars working in either direction.' HR/2'-class car No 1869, bound for Savoy Street, has pulled up to allow 'E/1' No 577, bound for Abbey Wood, to pass. *J.C. Gillham*

69

Above: Londoners throng alongside the tram tracks to bid farewell to tram 1863 as, with destination blind now missing, motorman T. Monk and conductor A. E. Harris crew the very last London Transport tram to leave the Embankment. *London Transport*

they headed up Wellington Street behind the Floral Hall of Covent Garden Market, where they found a small restaurant — 'Le Bon Viveur'. Despite its exotic French name it suffered from the restrictions and shortages prevalent in a still-rationed Britain, having a very restricted menu. Richard and John thought themselves quite lucky to be able to order liver and bacon with two vegetables, which they ate accompanied by a bottle of *vin rosé* — the only apparent concession to the restaurant's Gallic name. Suet pudding dessert followed, after which they lingered, chatting over cups of coffee. The conversation turned to London Transport's collection of preserved vehicles, which were stored at Reigate garage. John wondered whether they would ever be put on permanent display in the future.

'Can't ever see it,' said Richard. 'I mean, can you imagine a transport museum in Central London, say where we are now, in Covent Garden? It'd never happen.'

Their meals cost 4/3d each, with an extra 5/- for the bottle of wine. Richard offered to pay, giving the waiter a 10/- note and two half crown pieces whilst telling him

to keep the change. They left the restaurant just after 10pm and headed back down to the Embankment.

The long goodbye

The scene at the Embankment was transformed. Hundreds of people lined the tram tracks, the good-humoured crowd being supervised by police officers. Young and old, school children, teenagers, mothers, fathers and grandparents mixed together as London's last trams left the Embankment. Many in the crowd laid pennies on the tram rail to be kept as mementos after being bent by tram wheels. Souvenir-hunters had been at work on the trams themselves, almost all now stripped of stencils, blinds and indeed anything readily removable. Richard and John saw a policeman prevent a couple of youths attempting to remove the LT flag from the tram stop. With licensing hours closing the pubs at 11 o'clock, the crowds swelled ever larger, some needing to travel home on the trams, others wanting a last ride, while yet more simply stood and watched. Spontaneous

Above: Besieged by crowds and the Press, London's official Last Tram, No 1951, unloads passengers inside New Cross depot. *London Transport*

singing broke out, interspersed by loud cheers as each tram made its final journey along the Embankment.

Richard and John became a bit worried at the prospect of making it back to New Cross. Joining the tightly-packed throng on the riverward side of the Embankment, they held back as each packed tramcar passed, wanting to catch the very last tram. Just after 11.30pm the crowd surged forward as, to an extra-loud cheer, 'HR/2'-class car No 1863 on route 40 completed the crossover at Savoy Street and pulled up to the stop. Richard and John started to move forward involuntarily, pushed by the queue. The tram seemed packed already as they edged forward towards the entrance, where, grabbing a handrail, Richard and John pulled themselves onto the platform just before two LT inspectors blocked the entrance, the policeman with them saying: 'Sorry — no room for any more!'.

Seeing that the lower deck was choc-a-bloc with standing passengers, Richard and John went upstairs. The upper deck was almost as crowded, with many passengers standing and leaning out of windows.

Richard and John found a small standing-space by a seat stanchion and hung on as 1863 became the very last tram to leave the Embankment and cross Westminster Bridge. The car remained full to capacity throughout its final run, leaving many intending passengers amongst the crowds witnessing this journey through Kennington, Camberwell and Peckham disappointed at not being able to board. The journey should have taken 33min, but, delayed by the crowd, 1863 reached New Cross 18min late, at 12.29am on Sunday 6 July. Inspectors, who had remained on board throughout the journey, told passengers that the tram had reached journey's end. With feelings of regret and sadness doubtless shared by many other passengers, Richard and John left the last London tram on which they would travel. Once it was empty, one of the inspectors signalled to the driver, who notched up for the last time as 1863 headed towards Penhall Road and oblivion.

Richard and John elbowed their way through the crowd of onlookers. Each tram's arrival was greeted by a loud cheer, souvenir-hunters searching for any few

Right: The photographer's quick reactions allowed him to capture the only known shot of what is generally recognised as LT's last passenger-carrying tram journey. Bereft of blinds, No 187 catches the dispersing crowds by surprise upon its arrival at New Cross in the early hours of Sunday 6 July 1952.
C. Carter

remaining trophies before inspectors despatched each car on its final journey. Recognising the familiar face of Prince Marshall, Richard and John squeezed their way through the throng towards him. Prince told them that 'E/3'-class car No 1952 — obviously selected for the coincidence of its fleetnumber with calendar year — had already arrived from Charlton Works with the official London Transport party aboard, which included the Chairman (Lord Latham) and members of the Executive, the Chairman of London County Council, mayors of nine South London boroughs, and LT officers. At 1.00am the crowd had swelled still further — estimates put it at 20,000-strong — as the air of expectation increased.

The last scheduled car would be working route 40 from Woolwich Perrot Street to New Cross Gate and was already over half an hour late. Rumours began to circulate: 'Been cancelled because of the danger to the crowd'; 'Sent straight to Penhall Road'; 'Broken down'.

Richard and John were beginning to wonder whether they had already seen their last London tram in service when a roar from the crowd dispelled their doubts. 'E/3'-class car No 1951 crested the bridge over New Cross Gate station, arriving outside the depot at 1.15am. The Deputy Chairman of London Transport, John Cliff — a former tramway man — took over the controls from Driver Albert Fuller. Mr Cliff edged the car forward towards the depot, but its progress was soon halted by the huge crowds. Policemen and LT inspectors forced a gap through the good-natured throng, one policeman signalling to John Cliff to move the car forward. Notching up the controller brought no response — ironically LT's last tram in public service had become stuck on a dead section of conduit. The crowd behind 1951, realising what had happened, pushed the car, which soon regained power before

slowing as it passed into New Cross depot and history.

For a while Richard, John and Prince Marshall waited outside the depot. The crowds began to disperse as the three friends walked along New Cross Road. Suddenly there was a flurry of activity, with people running and some trying to get packed cameras out of bags, followed by the completely unexpected sound of tram wheels on track. Former Leyton Corporation 'E/3'-class car No 187 hove into view bound for New Cross, working the last route 72 journey from Woolwich via Eltham, which had been so delayed by crowds that it proved to be the actual last tram in public service, arriving after the official 'last tram'.

'Did you get a photograph of 187?' Prince Marshall asked a photographer.

'Yes, I think I did,' replied Nick Carter, 'on my trusty Ensign Selfix.'

'You'll probably be the only one that did. Well done. Fancy that — the actual last London tram being one of the Corporation cars rather than a London County Council one!'

They waited as inspectors outside New Cross depot supervised 187's reversal before its despatch to Penhall Road. Prince Marshall asked Richard and John what they planned to do next. They explained that they would have liked to go on to Penhall Road and then Abbey Wood to see the first bus run-out but were not sure how to get there, as hardly any Night Bus routes ran on a Saturday night / Sunday morning, and, in any case, none covered that road. 'Don't worry,' said Prince. 'You can come along with me. I've got a prewar Austin Seven Ruby motor car.'

After getting into Prince's car, parked in Goodwood Road (off New Cross Road), they set off along near-deserted streets, passing through Greenwich and reaching Penhall Road at around 2.30am. On that warm

Above: An arc light shines on two of the seven 'E/3'-class cars retained at New Cross depot for a short while in the early hours of Sunday 6 July for filming in conjunction with the British Transport Commission's memorable film on London's trams, *The Elephant Will Never Forget. J. C. Gillham*

night a small knot of dedicated enthusiasts stood around the entrance to the yard; inside, a line of tramcars fresh out of service was being moved one by one on the traverser into neat rows.

Just after 3.00am they heard the sound of wheels on metal down Woolwich Road, from which direction an impressive spectacle hove into view as a line of seven 'E/3'-class cars — those that had been kept behind at New Cross depot for the BTC film unit — approached in convoy. As the procession reached Penhall Road an inspector switched the points, and the first car entered. Stopping whilst its trolley pole was raised to temporary overhead wiring in the yard, the car then shot its very last 'plough' before inching forward for the last time under its own power towards the traverser. The other six cars followed in turn, last of all being No 1931, one of the two cars hired by the Light Railway Transport League for its farewell tour. Then a workman pulled a rope across the entrance, leaving the small group outside contemplating the rows of tramcars — now silenced forever — visible in the dappled moonlight.

A few minutes later, the group headed back to Prince Marshall's Austin car. Passing through Woolwich, they made for Abbey Wood. Richard, sitting in the back, suddenly felt very tired and dozed off to sleep. As they entered Plumstead High Street, the jolt of the car's wheels, running on the cobble setts between the now-redundant tramcar tracks, woke him up with a start.

'Do you know,' he said, 'I had the most extraordinary dream. It was some time in the future. Maybe about fifty years from now. I think I was in Croydon. The streets seemed much the same, although the shops looked different and there were lots of tall buildings — rather like skyscrapers. But the strangest thing was that there were trams running there. Not like the London ones we know, though — these were all single-deckers, continental-looking.' He paused for a few seconds, contemplating his dream, before adding: 'I wonder if that will ever happen?'

John smiled. 'Only in your dreams, Richard. Trams are finished in London.'

Omnibus victorious

Amid wisps of early-morning mist drifting up from the Thames Estuary, Prince Marshall parked his car in Abbey Wood Road just after 4.15am, and the trio crossed to the LT garage, joining a small group of enthusiasts already gathered near the entrance. Glancing inside, they could see that the tramway traverser was still in use for parking up buses in line. A few minutes later the traverser moved along the line of buses, after which RTL3 emerged onto the forecourt with blinds set for route 182. Richard noticed that this bus carried the running plate AW2, indicating that it should be the second (not the first) bus to work out of Abbey Wood garage. He approached the nearby garage inspector and raised this query.

The inspector consulted his duty schedule and uttered a mild expletive. 'They've brought the wrong bus out. Should be RTL25 on duty AW1. Probably that one's blocked in and couldn't get to the traverser. Too late now, anyway. RTL3 will have to go out first. Have to try to swap the running plates out on the road later on. What a mix-up!'

'Are we allowed to go on RTL3 to Woolwich?' Richard asked the inspector.

'Don't know about that,' came the reply. 'It runs out

Above: In mid-1952 the Government put pressure on industry to give priority to export orders, in order to reduce the country's balance of trade deficit. This dried up supplies of new buses, and consequently many of the buses used in Stage 8 of Operation Tramaway were prewar STL and RT types — not much younger than many of the trams they replaced. 'Prewar' RT124 (FXT 299) stands outside the Harrow Inn at Abbey Wood on the first day's operation of route 177, which replaced tram routes 36/38 to the Embankment. Officially allocated to New Cross garage, this bus was one of a number temporarily operated from Peckham garage, until the rebuilding of New Cross from tram depot to bus garage was completed. The bus displays an experimental three-line intermediate destination blind introduced at this time, which sacrificed the comprehensive listings possible on the usual five-line display for greater clarity. *C. Carter*

Below: 'H1B'-class trolleybus No 766B (ELB 766) was one of a number of trolleybuses damaged or destroyed as a result of enemy action at Bexleyheath depot in June 1944. Its leyland chassis was rebodied by East Lancashire Coach Builders in 1946, the suffix letter being added to its fleetnumber to indicate this. It is seen in Parson's Hill, Woolwich — the terminus of trolleybus routes 696 to Dartford and 698 to Bexleyheath, which operated in physical isolation from the rest of LT's trolleybus network. *C. Carter*

Above: Watched by an LT officer, garage staff, crews and a handful of enthusiasts, 1948-built RTL3 (JXN 315), bearing AW2 running plates, works what is described in LT Museum records as the 'first bus out of Abbey Wood garage' on Sunday 6 July 1952. When making up the destination blinds for Abbey Wood's new bus routes, the printer inadvertently included on them instructions for crews as to their use. When this error was realised, such details were painted over, resulting in the blank space after the final destination. *London Transport*

of service to Woolwich. Not sure . . . not sure at all, he continued, shaking his head. 'The Top Brass is here this morning. Being London Transport, an officer always comes to make sure that everything is going smoothly on a big changeover. I'll have to ask him,' he continued, approaching a tall gentleman wearing a bowler hat.

The two conferred for a short while, after which the man in the bowler hat glanced across at the three friends. 'I've seen you before, haven't I?' he asked Prince Marshall. 'don't you work at Ian Allan's transport bookshop in Vauxhall Bridge Road?'

'Yes, sir,' replied Prince.

'I thought so. I must say Ian Allan publish some very worthwhile transport books and magazines.' Turning to the inspector, he added: 'They look like sensible enthusiasts to me. You can let them ride on RTL3 to Woolwich. After all, it's a rather special journey, isn't it?'

The three friends thanked the officer and inspector before boarding RTL3, and at 4.31am, with dawn breaking, the Leyland Titan pulled away from Abbey Wood, following the line of the now-redundant tram tracks through Plumstead, to reach Woolwich 10 minutes later; there it manœuvred onto the new bus stand at General Gordon Place for tramway-replacement bus routes terminating in Woolwich. After waiting a couple of minutes the conductor rang the bell at 4.33am and RTL3 set off along roads worked the previous day by tram routes 44 and 46 to Eltham.

As they travelled, Prince Marshall explained to

Richard and John that Abbey Wood garage worked just three turns on route 182 on Sundays only, when the garage had buses surplus from its main weekday allocation for route 177. New Cross garage carried the main allocation for both routes, but, to complicate matters further, its vehicles for these routes were temporarily kept at Peckham garage, as New Cross was still undergoing a major rebuild from tram depot to bus garage. He went on to explain that LT had placed an embargo on the withdrawal of STL-class buses since April 1952, with the aims of increasing fleet size to cover the final tramway-conversion programme, of allowing for expected growth in traffic and of building up a reserve to cover anticipated extra demand in Coronation Year (1953).

The journey on route 182 was a short working which turned at Eltham Well Hall station. After a 5min layover, the Leyland Titan set off back to Woolwich at 5.04am. Crossing Shooters Hill, RTL3 passed RTL25 (which had been extricated from Abbey Wood garage) working the next outward 182 journey, and at 5.20am pulled up again in General Gordon Place, where the trio alighted. By now, all three were feeling hungry. Heading to Market Hill, they were relieved to find that the Vermont Café was open. Seated in its smoky atmosphere amidst early-morning dock workers, they tucked into fried breakfasts washed down with hot sweet tea. After finishing their breakfasts, which cost them 9d each, they left and sat down on a bench near the

Above: At the entrance to Penhall Road Yard on Sunday 6 July 1952, a knot of enthusiasts observe and record the sombre scene as rows of tramcars, which only the previous day had banged and clanged their way through the streets of South East London, stand silent awaiting their fate. In the foreground may be seen a cut-down snowbroom car and a Fordson tractor used to shunt the cars. *C. Carter*

Above: STL930 (CGJ 67) crosses Westminster Bridge against the backdrop of County Hall, from where London County Council administered the capital. This 1935-built bus — barely younger than elements of the replaced tramcar fleet — is working route 163, which replaced tram route 40. Although officially allocated to New Cross garage, the bus was temporarily operated from Camberwell garage pending completion of New Cross's rebuilding. *G. W. Morant*

Woolwich Free Ferry. Fatigue quickly overcame them and all three fell asleep.

At 7 o'clock they were woken by a siren of a cargo ship, heading up the River Thames to London Docks, crossing the path of the Woolwich Free Ferry. As Prince Marshall needed to return to his car at Abbey Wood, Richard and John said that they would come along with him so that they could see the garage in daylight. Walking to Beresford Square, at 7.24am they boarded 'prewar' RT43 on route 177 travelling the now familiar road to Abbey Wood. Once there, Prince Marshall bade his farewell, hoping that they would meet up again before too long. After looking at the garage and operations for a while, Richard and John boarded another 'prewar' RT, RT94, again on route 177. Setting off on this at 8.27am, the pair travelled through Woolwich and alighted at Penhall Road Yard. Richard and John spent about an hour here chatting with other enthusiasts grouped around the entrance to the yard containing lines of London's now-redundant trams.

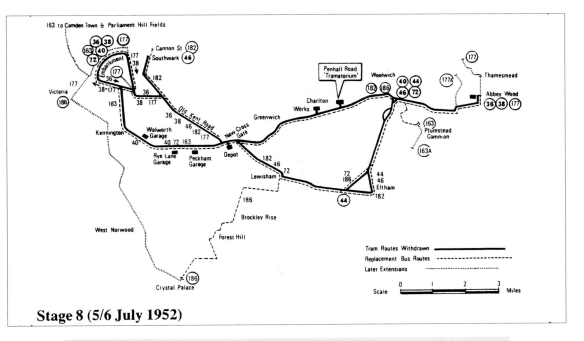

Stage 8 (5/6 July 1952)

Operation Tramaway Stage 8 (5/6 July 1952)

Tram routes withdrawn	Replacement bus routes
36 Abbey Wood–Embankment loop via Blackfriars	177 Abbey Wood–Embankment via either Blackfriars or Westminster loop
38 Abbey Wood–Embankment loop via Westminster	(via Westminster to Horse Guards Avenue on Saturday afternoon and Sundays)
40 Woolwich*–Savoy Street (*Plumstead weekday peak hours)	163 Plumstead Common–Horse Guards Avenue
44 Woolwich–Eltham (Weekdays only)	182 Woolwich–Cannon Street
46 Woolwich–Southwark Bridge	
72 Woolwich–Savoy Street	186 Woolwich–Crystal Palace (diverted at Lewisham to take over western half of bus 94)

Related alterations were also made to bus routes 21, 21A, 94, 161, 179, 180 as well as the withdrawal of bus route 53 (Greenwich–Plumstead Common)

The day had become very humid, and the effects of this, combined with well over 24 hours without proper sleep, and the physical demands imposed by almost continuous travelling or standing, were taking their toll; Richard and John knew that they had to return home. At 10am they boarded RTL55 on route 177, leaving that bus at New Cross Gate. Here they took a last look at the former tramway depot, the scene of such exciting 'last tram' activity less than 12 hours earlier. Just after 11 o'clock they waited at the stop for route 163 and considered themselves a bit lucky when STL474 pulled up; STLs were only officially allocated to the route on Mondays-Fridays, so probably a shortage of vehicles had caused this one to be turned out on a Sunday. Travelling as far as Westminster, they got off at the Embankment stop and walked the short distance into Whitehall. Here, at 11.36am, they boarded RTW117 on route 11 to travel to Victoria Coach Station in Buckingham Palace Road. Heading back to Reading on Thames Valley route B, the tired pair reflected that they had indeed seen history in the making.

Journey schedule

Saturday 5 July 1952

Terminus	Dep/Arr	Route No	Vehicle	Garage Allocation	Fare
Embankment (Westminster) Elephant & Castle	10.00am 10.08am	36	'E/3' 1923	New Cross	3d
Elephant & Castle Embankment (Savoy Street)	10.17am 10.29am	36	'E/3' 1948	New Cross	3d
Embankment (Savoy Street) Old Kent Road (Bricklayers Arms)	10.31am 10.45am	36	'E/3' 1948	New Cross	3d
Old Kent Road (Bricklayers Arms) Southwark Bridge	11.09am 11.14am	46	'E/1' 341 *	Abbey Wood	2d
Southwark Bridge Woolwich (Beresford Square)	11.42am 12.46pm	46	'E/1' 83 §	Abbey Wood	11d
Woolwich (Beresford Square) Abbey Wood	1.02pm 1.17pm	38	'E/1' 592	Abbey Wood	3d
Abbey Wood Woolwich (Beresford Square)	2.14pm 2.29pm	36	'E/3' 1923	New Cross	3d
Woolwich (Beresford Square) Eltham (Middle Park Avenue)	3.13pm 3.30pm	72	'HR/2' 1859	New Cross	5d
Eltham (Middle Park Avenue) Woolwich (Beresford Square)	4.17pm 4.38pm	44	'E/1' 307 *	Abbey Wood	5d
Woolwich (Beresford Square) Embankment (Savoy Street)	6.50pm 7.53pm	40	'E/3' 168 $	New Cross	11d
Embankment (Savoy Street) New Cross Gate	11.38pm 12.29am	40	'HR/2' 1863	New Cross	5d

* ex-West Ham   § ex-East Ham $ ex-Leyton

Journey schedule

Sunday 6 July 1952

Terminus	Dep/Arr	Route No	Vehicle	Garage Allocation	Fare
Abbey Wood Garage Woolwich (General Gordon Pl)	4.31am 4.41am	(out of service)	RTL3	AW	(none taken)
Woolwich (General Gordon Pl) Eltham (Well Hall Station)	4.43am 4.59am	182	RTL3	AW	3d
Eltham (Well Hall Station) Woolwich (General Gordon Pl)	5.04am 5.20am	182	RTL3	AW	3d
Woolwich (Beresford Square) Abbey Wood Garage	7.24am 7.37am	177	RT43	NX (PM)	3d
Abbey Wood Garage Charlton (Penhall Road Yard)	8.27am 8.50am	177	RT94	NX (PM)	5d
Charlton (Penhall Road Yard) New Cross Gate	10.00am 10.17am	177	RTL55	AW	6d
New Cross Gate Embankment (Westminster)	11.07am 11.28am	163	STL474	NX (Q)	6d
Westminster (Whitehall) Buckingham Palace Rd (Victoria Coach Stn)	11.36am 11.42am	11	RTW117	D	3d

6

Rides alongside the Royal River

THE first Monday in August was traditionally designated as August Bank Holiday. Richard and John decided to use that day to make a journey around London Transport operations in West and South West London. They hoped that the trip would enable them to travel on a new 'Q1' trolleybus, as well as sampling some vintage and utility buses which were not expected to remain in passenger service for much longer. The pair set off from Reading at 7am aboard Thames Valley 590, one of a number of Bristol KS6B double-deckers with Eastern Coach Works lowbridge bodywork fitted with coach seats and platform doors especially for use on the London services. The double-decker on limited-stop route B made good progress, following the A4 Bath Road through Maidenhead, where it crossed the River Thames, to Slough. At Slough the Bristol entered the London Passenger Transport Area. Richard explained to John that the LPTA boundary was a bit like the Iron Curtain: LT did not cross west of Slough and

Thames Valley did not cross to its east — except for route B, which, because of its origins as an independent service introduced in 1929, had exceptionally been granted a London Transport 'consent' to run in the area.

Past Heath Row

Passing through Slough, where plenty of Country Area vehicles were to be seen, route B paralleled the only Central Area bus route to reach Slough — the 81 from Hounslow — as well as Green Line routes 704 and 705 from Windsor to Tunbridge Wells and Sevenoaks respectively. *En route* through Colnbrook, with its centuries-old coaching inns which echoed the Bath Road's long history, an RT double-decker on route 81 and an almost brand-new RF coach on the 705, duplicated by a Windsor-based RT double-decker fully laden with passengers bound for a day out in Windsor, squeezed past the Bristol in the narrow High Street.

Left: Seen in pristine Country Area bus livery following a full overhaul in May 1952, 1935-built STL1743 (DGX 282) was one of a number of buses so treated in furtherance of LT's policy to increase overall fleet size. The bus is seen on layover against the backdrop of Windsor Castle. Route 417 was one of a number of bus and Green Line coach routes serving the three-mile stretch of road between Windsor and Slough via Eton High Street — one of the most intensively-served roads in the Country Area, with (on weekdays) over 300 journeys a day in each direction. This high level of service was partly attributable to the high incidence of positioning journeys from Windsor garage. *D. Morris, courtesy T. W. Moore*

BRITISH EUROPEAN AIRWAYS

London Transport had assumed the contract to operate BEA's London terminal passenger coach service on 16 July 1947. During 1952, services operated from the terminal at Kensington Air Station at Stafford Court in High Street, Kensington, to London (Heath Row) and Northolt airports. The coaches, owned by BEA, operated from LT's Victoria (Gillingham Street) garage.

Right: The first-generation BEA coaches are exemplified by 1947-built Commer Avenger SME 537, seen having just entered London Airport from the Bath Road. The $1\frac{1}{2}$-deck Park Royal body design was developed in collaboration with BEA's immediate predecessor, the European Division of British Overseas Airways Corporation, to mirror airline travel of the time, which was exclusive, expensive and luxurious. Only 18 passengers were carried, on double offside and single nearside seats. The rear part of the coach was raised above a luggage space of 180cu ft capacity access to which was through twin rear doors which could be sealed for Customs purposes. The central passenger entrance and separate emergency door are clearly visible in this shot. *J.C.Gillham*

Above: As aircraft capacities increased, the 18-seat Commers proved increasingly uneconomical. Replacement coaches again had specialised bodywork developed jointly by Park Royal and London Transport. Retaining some features from the Commers (split-level passenger compartment with rear seats raised above a large luggage space, and central doorway), the 37-seat coachwork incorporated a flat roof design mounted on an underfloor-engined AEC Regal IV chassis. Whilst these vehicles were still owned by BEA, LT became the 'registered keeper' for motor-taxation purposes, resulting in the use of registration numbers from blocks reserved for LT, rather than Middlesex numbers as had been the case previously. MLL 717 is seen outside Gillingham Street garage in the company of RF5/6 (LUC 205/6), which have their destination blinds set for Tour No 6 (St Albans and Hatfield House) and Tour No 3 (Windsor and Hampton Court) respectively. *M.J.Dryhurst*

Above: The 100-strong, 1937-built 'F1' class of all-Leyland LPTB70 trolleybuses, exemplified by 684 (DLY 684), passing along Chiswick High Road, had a long association with Hanwell depot. Route 655 had a daily core service between Hammersmith and Hanwell. Peak-hour projections at each end (from Hammersmith to Clapham Junction and from Hanwell to Acton) combined to create the system's longest through journey time for a trolleybus route, taking 1hr 17min — a distinction shared with route 630, which covered a common section with route 655 between Hammersmith and Wandsworth. *R. H. G. Simpson*

A few miles further on, passengers craned to look out of the windows at the sight of a BOAC de Havilland Comet — the world's first commercial jet airliner — taking-off from an airfield to the south of the Bath Road. Shortly afterwards, the bus passed a collection of wartime huts and other temporary buildings which acted as the terminal for London Airport. John, who had good knowledge of aviation matters from his RAF days, explained to Richard that London Airport had originally been a World War 2 airfield at a place known as Heath Row (in later years contracted to 'Heathrow'). On 31 May 1946 it had been officially handed over for use by civilian flights, being designated as the new London Airport.

Continuing along the Bath Road and then down the Great West Road, the friends saw airline coaches in the blue and cream livery of British Overseas Airways Corporation and two-tone grey of British European Airways heading for London Airport carrying passengers from the airlines' central-London terminals. After following the Great West Road for about 5 miles, the Bristol double-decker negotiated a busy roundabout junction with the North and South Circular roads and headed into Chiswick High Road.

W4 to W5 via W3

To the north, the 31-acre site of London Transport's Chiswick Works came into view. Richard explained to

John that this had been built in 1922 by the London General Omnibus Co to centralise major overhauls of its 4,000-vehicle bus fleet at one site. Despite subsequent extensions to Chiswick Works, the growth in size of LT's bus fleet — 8,477 buses and coaches were owned at 1 January 1952 — meant that the workload had come to exceed Chiswick's capacity. Thus after World War 2 an unused Underground railway depot at Aldenham had been developed to take some of the workload. It was planned that Aldenham would ultimately become the centre for major overhauls of buses, with Chiswick being responsible for work on electrical and mechanical assemblies. In 1952, however, they shared the various functions.

Richard and John left the Thames Valley bus in Chiswick High Road at 8.41am. The day was now sunny and warm, although clouds heralded the prospect of heavy showers. They walked along Chiswick High Road watching the variety of vehicles on the three trolleybus and four Green Line coach routes serving the thoroughfare. A little further along they found Turnham Green bus garage, whose entire allocation consisted of RT-class double-deckers. The next route that they wanted to travel on was the 55, and, after finding the stop, they were pleased to see STL448 — one of Southall garage's few remaining examples of this class — approaching. After boarding they went upstairs, taking the rear upper-deck seat. The conductor collected

81

their 8d fares as the bus weaved through residential streets and then into Acton High Street, which it followed for ¼ mile before heading southeast down Gunnersbury Lane, passing Acton Town station and crossing the North Circular Road into Gunnersbury Park. Richard recognised the man who boarded here and came upstairs.

'Hello John!' he said. 'How are you?'

'Fine, thank you,' replied John Gillham, a well-respected enthusiast who was a contributor to Ian Allan's *Buses Illustrated* as well as the author of the publisher's recently-issued *London's Double-Deck Buses*. 'I live along here,' he continued. 'I'm just off to West Ealing. What are you chaps up to?'

Richard explained their travel plans for the day.

'Your luck might be in,' John rejoined. 'It looks as if LT are set on withdrawing all their utility buses as soon as possible. Route 97 still has Bristol Utilities allocated to it on weekdays from Southall garage. The official Sunday and Bank Holiday allocation is RT class but I expect that, because today is a Bank Holiday, some of the RTs will be out on excursions, so you may well find some Bristols pressed into service. Won't be many more chances to ride these vehicles in London. I'll tell you another thing: if you can get to Esher today you might find RTC1 out on the 416. That's another bus that won't be in service for much longer, so I've heard.'

All three alighted from STL448 at West Ealing, where John Gillham bade farewell and went on his way. Richard and John walked along Uxbridge Road towards Ealing Broadway, watching the frequent passage of trolleybuses on route 607. Bus route 97, with a 12min frequency on Sunday/Bank Holiday mornings, also used Uxbridge Road, and the friends watched keenly for each bus, but, every time, their hope

of seeing a utility Bristol was dashed by the appearance of one of Southall garage's RT class. After a while they reached the 97 stop at Haven Green, outside Ealing Broadway station. Knowing that they had to press on with their journey, the pair decided to catch the next southbound 97, expecting yet another RT. Their hearts leapt when they saw the profile of a utility Duple-bodied Bristol K6A drawing closer, until B18 pulled up at the stop. They boarded, getting a seat midway along the upper deck. As the bus moved off, they heard the smooth tones of its 7.7-litre AEC engine — a sound characteristic of London buses such as the STL — although they realised that the four-speed crash gearbox was much less sophisticated than the preselector transmissions fitted to many of LT's buses and coaches. Having passed Northfields station and along Windmill Road, the Bristol reached its terminus at Half Acre in Brentford at 11.14am.

To Hampton Court by trolleybus

Leaving the Bristol, Richard and John walked into the nearby High Street. Local traffic on this thoroughfare was catered for exclusively by trolleybus routes 655, 657 and 667. They knew that the first vehicles from a batch of 50 new 'Q1'-class trolleybuses had entered service from 1 June from Fulwell depot on route 667. In the High Street they watched the almost continual passage of trolleybuses, many of which were 1935/6 'C1'-class AEC 664Ts with Weymann or Metro-Cammell bodies — LT's first batch of long-wheelbase, three-axle, 70-seat trolleybuses, which became the standard size for the system. Richard and John had decided to catch the first southbound 'Q1' trolleybus they saw on route 667. Seeing No 1844 approaching the stop, they joined the

Right: London Transport's utility Bristols were associated with Southall garage (renamed from Hanwell in 1950 upon the formation of Central Road Services, to avoid confusion with similarly-named Hanwell trolleybus depot), where they spent the greater part of their lives in the Metropolis. B18 (HGC 243), seen passing through Ealing Broadway, was one of 20 K6As received in 1945 with Duple bodies built to the 'relaxed austerity' style by then permitted by the Ministry of Supply. *J.C.Gillham*

ROUTE 667 TROLLEYBUSES AT HAMPTON COURT

Route 667, from Hammersmith to Hampton Court, had been converted from tram to trolleybus operation on 27 October 1935 in London Transport's first such scheme, involving former London United Tramways routes in West London. With a 55min through journey time, the route enjoyed an enhanced (4min) headway on Summer Sundays and Bank Holidays, on these occasions requiring 29 trolleybuses from Fulwell depot.

Left: The 90-strong, 1939/40-built 'N1'-class trolleybuses, based on AEC 664T chassis, were associated primarily with Bow depot, but two of these vehicles — Nos 1565A and 1587A — spent many years working from Fulwell. Both had had their original bodies destroyed by enemy action at Bow depot; the separate incidents, in September 1940 and March 1941, reflect the onslaught to which London's East End was subjected by the Luftwaffe during the height of the Blitz. Both vehicles were rebodied by Weymann in 1942, being reclassified as Class N1A and gaining the 'A' suffix to their fleetnumbers. No 1587A (FXH 587) is seen on layover in Hampton Court Road. *C. Carter*

Right: In pristine condition, having been delivered only in June 1952, 'Q1'-class Metro-Cammell-bodied BUT 9641T trolleybus No 1852 (LYH 852) — part of London Transport's final intake of new trolleybuses — stands at the same spot as No 1587A above. *C. Carter*

Right: The unique 'X7'-class trolleybus of 1939, No 1671 (DTD 649), is seen passing along Kew Bridge Road, Brentford, on route 655. As its Lancashire registration suggests, this chassisless, twin-steer trolleybus, resembling the contemporary Leyland-built 'K' class, was originally a demonstrator with Leyland Motors, being acquired by LT in September 1939. The design concept was an attempt to reduce the damage to tyres and road surfaces caused by conventional, rigid-twin-axle (bogie) designs when cornering. *J. C. Gillham*

queue and, after boarding, went upstairs. The trolleybus was well laden, mostly with families intent on a day out at Hampton Court. There were no empty pairs of seats, so Richard and John sat on vacant seats beside the gangway. The 'Q1' accelerated away smoothly, and the conductor came upstairs to collect their 11d fares as the trolleybus passed Syon Park. After loading at Twickenham, 1844 was full to capacity, the conductor giving a three-bell ring to indicate this to his driver. A duplicate trolleybus was parked in King Street, where they saw its conductor standing ready with a 'bamboo' pole to put its trolley arms back onto the overhead once 1844 had passed. No 1844 continued non-stop — it seemed all passengers were for Hampton Court. As they passed Fulwell depot, Richard recalled that London's first permanent trolleybus service had been started on 16 May 1931 by London United with 'A1'-class 'Diddlers' based at this depot. Negotiating the narrow streets of Hampton, Richard and John glimpsed the River Thames as 1844 turned left to reach Hampton Court, where it would terminate a few minutes later.

The crowds at Hampton Court on that Bank Holiday Monday were enormous. Some were attracted by the history and grounds of the Tudor palace with its famous Maze. Others had come to enjoy the River Thames, whilst yet more thronged to a funfair on the Green. Many of these visitors had travelled by London Transport, which ran enhanced services. Three bus routes — the 14A from Hornsey Rise, 27B from Archway and 112 from Palmers Green — had summer Sunday and Bank Holiday extensions to Hampton Court, bringing buses from distant North London garages (such as Chalk Farm, Cricklewood, Holloway and Willesden) much further south than they would normally venture.

Vintage bus rides

Richard and John spent half an hour watching the activity before heading for the bus stop in Vrow Walk. They wanted to travel on to Kingston, thinking that they would probably catch a 604 trolleybus, which ran every three minutes. They were about to board No 1839, from the first batch of 'Q1s', delivered to LT in 1948, when the sight of T9 working route 264 changed their minds for them. Boarding the 1929-built AEC Regal by its front entrance, they took seats halfway down the saloon. A conductress collected their 3d fares as the bus accelerated away. Richard told John that this batch of vehicles had been kept in service specially because of a weight restriction on Walton Bridge, over which routes 218 and 264 operated. The approach to Kingston Bridge was mightily congested, the pair admiring the Norbiton garage driver's mastery of the bus's crash gearbox as he perforce changed gear continually between first and second as the traffic crept hesitatingly forward. Gaining the Surrey side of the River Thames, the Regal entered Kingston-upon-Thames — the oldest of only three Royal Boroughs in England. Richard and John left the bus at its Wood Street terminus outside Kingston station.

It was now getting on for 1 o'clock, and the day had become warm, with a temperature approaching 70°F. Richard and John, who had been on the move since leaving Reading at 7am, needed some sustenance, this being provided by the Cadena Café. Refreshed, they departed that establishment with a short time left to watch bus operations in Kingston. They soon found Kingston bus garage, the front portion of which was used as a bus station. An inspector on duty noticed their interest and started talking to them. He explained that Kingston garage was hemmed in by other buildings and

REGAL VARIETY IN KINGSTON

Incredibly, the whole span of T-class development, from T1 built in 1929 to T798 dating from 1948, could be seen through vehicles still in London Transport service in 1952.

Above: T30 (UU 6645) entered service in December 1929 as one of a batch of 50 buses which comprised London General's first AEC Regals. The operator-built bodywork originally had a rear platform entrance but was rebuilt to front-entrance in 1933 and in the immediate postwar years was further rebuilt by Marshall Motor Bodies Ltd of Cambridge, a number of elderly LT buses being so treated. Finally an AEC diesel engine, taken from a scrapped STL, was fitted to replace its petrol original in 1950. Classified 1T1s, these were the lightest full-size saloons in LT's fleet, and 22 of them, including T30, continued in service during 1952 from Kingston and Norbiton garages to maintain routes 218 (Kingston–Staines) and 264 (Kingston–Hersham Green), both of which crossed Walton Bridge, which was subject to a weight restriction. The bus is seen at the setting-down stand in Kingston's Cromwell Road. *J.C.Gillham*

Left: T298 (GN 4672) entered service in 1931 as a Weymann-bodied Green Line coach. In 1938 it was one of 31 AEC Regals to receive 1935-built Weymann bus bodies removed from R-class AEC Reliance chassis, thus creating the 11T11 sub-class. The bus is seen in Ceres Road beside Kingston station on 26 April 1952, shortly before withdrawal. *J.C.Gillham*

Left: For many the 10T10 AEC Regals, built in 1938/9, represented the pinnacle of prewar LT vehicle design. With the advent of the Green Line RF coaches, a number were transferred for use on Central Area routes. Forty of these were specially modified for such use and were repainted in red livery; others were pressed into service still sporting Green Line livery, as exemplified by T531 (ELP 255) passing Kingston station. *J.C.Gillham*

Left: To obtain new vehicles at a time of great shortage, LT received in 1946 50 14T12 AEC Regals built to provincial standard. The Weymann bodywork echoed prewar design, whilst the use of sliding window vents was unique among LT buses at the time. T741 (HGF 831) is seen in Clarence Street, Kingston, in pale January 1952 sunshine when allocated to Kingston garage. Kingston's entire allocation of 14T12s was transferred to Norbiton garage when the latter opened on 14 May 1952. *Aviation & Transport Photographs, courtesy R.Marshall*

Above: Concurrent with the immediate postwar intake of standard provincial-specification T-class AEC Regals came two batches of Leyland Tiger PS1s, also built to provincial specification. The first batch, TD1-31, built in 1946/7, carried Weymann bodywork of similar style to that of contemporary T-class deliveries; the second batch of 100 buses, TD32-131, was received in 1948/9 bearing bodywork built by Mann Egerton of Norwich. TD70 (JXC 263), seen on the same January day as T741 (previous page), was one of 11 such buses allocated to Kingston garage in 1952, principally for route 216 (Kingston–Staines). *Aviation & Transport Photographs, courtesy R. Marshall*

could not be expanded. Its allocation had become so large that, until the opening of LT's fourth new postwar garage, at Norbiton on 14 May 1952, 38 Kingston buses had had to be parked overnight off the premises, many on nearby railway land. The new Norbiton garage had since taken over operation of several Kingston routes.

At 1.45pm another 1929-vintage AEC Regal — T11 — pulled into Kingston Bus Station on route 218 to Staines. Two minutes later the bus set off, heading out of Kingston along the Portsmouth Road, which runs parallel with the River Thames through The Dittons. The road traffic had increased markedly by the time the route joined the A3 Kingston By-pass at the Scilly Isles roundabout. After passing Sandown Park Racecourse the AEC headed into Esher, where Richard and John left it at 2.06pm near the Windsor Arms in the High Street.

Through genteel Surrey

Mindful of John Gillham's earlier advice, they waited in the High Street, and were delighted when at 2.19pm they saw RTC1 approaching on route 416 and park up in the yard of the Windsor Arms. Richard and John had a chance for a quick inspection of this unusual bus before it set off back to Leatherhead after a short (3min) layover. Feeling thirsty, they went into the Windsor

Arms where they enjoyed refreshing glasses of shandy before the landlord called 'time' at 2.30pm.

Richard's and John's next objective was Weybridge, served by route 219, to which Kingston garage allocated both T- and Q-class saloons. They particularly wished to travel on a Q-class bus, knowing that these revolutionary-for-their-day side-engined vehicles built in 1935/6 would not remain in service for much longer. The first westbound bus to appear on the 219 was a T, at 2.44pm. Letting that pass, they waited another 15 minutes, only to be disappointed to see another T arrive at 2.59pm. Looking at each other with exasperation, they decided to wait yet another 15 minutes for the next bus, agreeing to catch whatever turned up. In the interval, interest was provided by an RTL of Riverside garage, which turned up on route 72 to East Acton, and Green Line RF coach of Hertford, working route 715 to Guildford.

Before too long, Q65 approached on route 219. Richard and John boarded, taking seats halfway down, and the bus set off, the familiar tone of an AEC engine seeming to come from within the saloon. Through Hersham and towards Weybridge, the bus passed substantial villas set in tree-lined avenues. Richard guessed that they were now in what he had recently heard described, on BBC wireless's Third Programme (in what, he assumed, was an American idiom), as 'commuter land'. The bus pulled up at 'The Ship' in Weybridge

ESHER HIGH STREET

Right: From 1948 onwards, some of the Country Area's 1935-vintage 4Q4s were transferred to the Central Area. Whilst a few were repainted into red livery, most commenced their new rôle still sporting Country Area green and cream, as exemplified by Q13 (BXD 534). With a good complement of passengers, the bus is working lengthy 30min-frequency route 215 from Kingston, which largely followed the main A3 Portsmouth road to Ripley — one of the furthest-flung Central Area termini. The bus's entrance door had to remain permanently in the open position in compliance with contemporary Metropolitan Police regulations, which forbade the use of closing doors on Central Area buses. The slipboard to the right of the door lists minimum fares applicable on the route, to discourage short-distance travel from Kingston. *J. C. Gillham*

Above: Experimental Green Line double-deck coach RTC1 (FXT 272) represented the third incarnation of 'prewar' RT97. Originally built in 1940, RT97 suffered bomb damage during the war. In 1946 it was rebuilt in conjunction with contemporary pay-as-you-enter trials, which involved a seated conductor. Once these were completed, RT97 entered the experimental shop at Chiswick Works, where its LPTB body was extensively rebuilt. From April 1949 the resultant RTC1 underwent evaluation on Green Line routes, but in December 1949 was relegated to bus duties from Leatherhead garage. It was usually to be found on route 416 from Leatherhead to Esher, where it is seen on layover in the yard of the 'Windsor Arms'. The full-width sloping bonnet, blending into the nearside wing, was clearly a precursor of the later Routemaster design. Experimental seats to 'airline standards' were fitted, and this was also the first LT bus to feature fluorescent lighting in the saloon and for the destination display. The platform step arrangement was a legacy from its trials as a pay-as-you-enter bus. *C. Carter*

High Street, where Richard and John alighted before it set off towards its terminus at the station.

Weybridge was served principally by the Country Bus & Coach Department, mostly with vehicles based at nearby Addlestone garage. Richard's and John's main reason for visiting the town was that routes 461, 461A and 463 were worked by lowbridge buses: services were maintained by a mixture of 1950 RLH-class AEC Regent IIIs and 1934 STL-class AEC Regents, supplemented by two 1930-vintage ST-class Regents. Richard and John knew that a further batch of 56 RLH-class AEC Regent IIIs was due for delivery in the autumn of 1952 which would mean the withdrawal of the lowbridge ST and STL types.

Whilst they were watching the bus activity a teenage boy came up to them, asking if they were interested in buses. 'I am, he said. 'My name's Michael Dryhurst. I'm dead keen on buses. I like photographing them, too.'

There was a pause in the conversation whilst the young man photographed RLH7. Richard then asked him if either of the STs was out on service that day. Michael replied that he had seen ST140 pass through, working a journey to Ottershaw at about 3.10pm, and that it should return fairly soon. Richard asked him what he planned to do when he left school.

'I'd like to be a bus designer — at Weymann's, just down the road from here, at Addlestone. It must be great, helping to build the latest buses for London

DRYHURST IN WEYBRIDGE, 1952

Right: Q65 (CGJ 170) was one of the former Country Area 4Q4s to be repainted into Central Area red livery. Operated on a 15min frequency, route 219 from Kingston featured peak-hour journeys projecting beyond Weybridge station to serve the Vickers works at Brooklands Aerodrome.
M.J.Dryhurst

Left: The first batch of 20 lowbridge RLH-class double-deckers was diverted to London Transport by the BTC in 1950 from Nottinghamshire-based Midland General Omnibus Co Ltd. Built to 'provincial' specification, these Weymann-bodied AEC Regent IIIs were fitted with wartime-style restricted front destination-blind displays. Addlestone garage's RLH7 (KYY 507) loads in St George's Hill, Weybridge.
M.J.Dryhurst

Right: Lowbridge Short Bros-bodied AEC Regent ST140 (GF 7214), converted from petrol to diesel engine in 1949, stands at St George's Hill, Weybridge, during its last days in London Transport service. It had started life in 1930 in the ownership of the National Omnibus & Transport Co.
M.J.Dryhurst

CARTER IN WALTON-ON-THAMES, 1952

Right: In 1934 the Country Bus & Coach Department received 12 new front-entrance lowbridge Weymann-bodied AEC Regents for use on route 410 (Bromley–Reigate), soon dubbed 'Godstone' STLs because of their allocation to that garage. Displaced from route 410 in 1950 by the arrival of new RLH-class buses, the 'Godstone' STLs were sent to Addlestone and Guildford garages for use on their lowbridge routes. STL1055 (BPF 458) departs Walton-on-Thames bound for Botleys Park on route 461A. *C. Carter*

Left: Seen in Bridge Street, Walton-on-Thames, 1929-built T9 (UU 6624) was rebuilt by Marshall in 1949 and was amongst those 1T1-type AEC Regals transferred from Kingston to Norbiton garage upon the latter's opening (on 14 May 1952) and assuming responsibility for route 264. *C. Carter*

Left: Walton-on-Thames Motor Co's 20-seat, Willmott-bodied Bedford WTB of 1937, DLD 407, departs Bridge Street bound for Walton station.
The continuation of this route in independent hands after the 1933 Act represented an anomaly in London Transport policy; although it lay outside the Metropolitan Police District (within the confines of which mandatory acquisition of all independent bus services was stipulated by the Act), it operated wholly within the London Special Area, within which London Transport policy was to negotiate to acquire any such operations. In contrast, other local bus services in Walton-on-Thames provided by Ben Stanley had been acquired by London Transport in April 1934. *C. Carter*

Journey schedule

Bank Holiday Monday 4 August 1952

Terminus	Dep/Arr	Route No	Vehicle	Garage Allocation	Fare
Reading Stations	7.00am	B *	590	Reading	3/3d
Chiswick High Road	8.41am				
Turnham Green	9.24am	55	STL448	HW	8d
West Ealing	9.51am				
Ealing Broadway (LT Station)	10.56am	97	B18	HW	5d
Brentford Half Acre	11.14am				
Brentford High Street	11.36am	667	'Q1' 1844	FW	11d
Hampton Court	12.10pm				
Hampton Court (Vrow Walk)	12.48pm	264	T9	NB	3d
Kingston Station	12.56pm				
Kingston Bus Station	1.47pm	218	T11	K	8d
Esher (Windsor Arms)	2.06pm				
Esher (Windsor Arms)	3.14pm	219	Q65	K	8d
Weybridge (The Ship)	3.35pm				
Weybridge (The Ship)	3.58pm	461A	ST140	WY	5d
Walton-on-Thames (Odeon)	4.10pm				
Walton-on-Thames (Walton Bridge)	5.26pm	218	T542	K	9d
Staines (Clarence Street)	5.53pm				
Staines Bridge	6.55pm	A *	677	Reading	3/-
Reading Stations	8.00pm				

* operated by Thames Valley Traction Co

Below: Not all 1T1 AEC Regals were rebuilt after World War 2. Although the bus was fitted with a second-hand diesel engine in 1950, the characteristic LGOC projecting waistline panel is the most obvious clue to the original condition of the bodywork of T156 (GF 7251). Seen in Esher Road, Hersham, T156 could lay claim to the distinction of being the first ever London General bus to be built with a front entrance when delivered in 1930. *J.C. Gillham*

Above: SRT160 (EGO 482) was the last of the ill-starred SRT class to be built before London Transport pulled the plug on the project at the end of 1949. Based on the chassis of 1937-built AEC Regent STL2438, the Park Royal-bodied RT lookalike, working out of Twickenham garage, is seen on layover in the forecourt of Staines West station on the 55min-long, 10min-frequency route 90 to Kew Gardens station. *A.B.Cross*

Transport and other operators.' He paused, reflecting for a few seconds before continuing: 'But the other day I thought about going into the film industry. That'd be exciting too! Meeting famous film stars — and I'd get to travel 'round the country and be able to see different bus operators. I might even get abroad, you know — perhaps even to America!' Looking up the road, he added: 'Here comes ST140.'

Richard and John said farewell to Michael Dryhurst before crossing the road in advance of the approaching ST. Looking back they saw Michael raise his camera to take a rear-offside shot. The two friends climbed upstairs, with Richard, who was 6ft tall, having to stoop to gain access to a bench seat halfway along the lowbridge body. The 22-year-old vintage AEC set off, its Short Bros body remarkably sound and rattle-free despite its age — a tribute to London Transport's standard of maintenance, thought Richard. Twelve minutes later they left ST140 in the pleasant little town of Walton-on-Thames, meeting point between Central and Country Areas the latter's contribution being principally the lowbridge routes already mentioned. Green Line routes 716 and 717 passed through with a combined 30min headway, worked since February 1952 by new RF coaches based at Addlestone, Hatfield and Hitchin

garages. Norbiton garage's RT-operated route 131 worked in from Kingston via the Moleseys. Two other Central Area bus routes passed through — the 218 (Kingston–Staines) and the 264 (Kingston–Hersham).

A local café provided welcome cups of tea, after which Richard and John walked to Walton Bridge. Earlier they had glimpsed a small Bedford WTB bus working in the town. They found this bus, belonging to Walton-on-Thames Motor Co, parked at the bridge, with its destination blind set for 'Walton Station'. Getting into conversation with its driver, they learned that the service to Walton station, about one mile beyond the town centre, was long-established. It ran mostly every half hour using just one bus, although at peak times during the week this was supplemented by other vehicles to provide a 10min service. After the Bedford set off at 5.10pm Richard and John lingered by the bridge, enjoying the late-afternoon sunshine. They bought 3d cornets from a Wall's ice-cream vendor and ate them whilst watching boats passing on the River Thames. Looking back towards the bus stop on the town side of the bridge, Richard and John saw T542 approach on route 218 bound for Staines. They boarded the 1938-built AEC Regal, one of 40 similar former coaches made redundant from Green Line work by the advent of new RF-class coaches and subsequently adapted for Central bus work in 1951/2. Despite the weight restriction, the bus crossed Walton Bridge and headed out into countryside. After going through Shepperton Village, T542 travelled along roads flanked by nurseries and market gardens before passing through Laleham and into Staines, where Richard and John left the bus in Clarence Street at 5.53pm.

Staines was another interesting town where Central and Country Area buses met, giving an interesting mix of services and vehicle types. These ranged from Central Area RTs (routes 116,117,162), SRTs (route 90), Ts (routes 216/218/224) and TDs (route 216) to Country Area STLs (routes 441D/469), RTs (routes 441/460), lowbridge RLHs and STLs (routes 436/436A/461) and Ts (routes 460/462). Green Line routes 701, 702 and 718 produced frequent sightings of new RF-class coaches. The pair walked to Staines West station to watch the variety of vehicle types on layover at one of the town's principal termini after which they went to a pub in nearby Church Street for a pint and a sandwich.

After nearly an hour in Staines it was time to head home. Richard and John walked across Staines Bridge, crossing the River Thames for the fourth time that day, and headed for the Green Line coach stop on the Egham side. Thames Valley's limited-stop route A from London to Reading also picked up here; Richard explained that this did not have LT consent because it was licensed as an express service, so could not carry local passengers within the LT area, unlike route B which could, being licensed as a stage-carriage service. At 6.55pm Thames Valley No 677, a brand-new Eastern Coach Works-bodied, underfloor-engined Bristol LS6G

pulled up, bound for Reading on route A. They boarded and sat down for a speedy journey home.

John asked Richard why LT did not buy Bristol chassis and ECW bodies now that they were ultimately controlled by the BTC. Richard replied that this was something London Transport would always have to look at — the 15 RFW-class coaches delivered in 1951 had been fitted with ECW bodies, and he had heard rumours that LT might evaluate a Bristol LS bus next year. However, he went on to explain that, under the terms of the 1933 Act, London Transport had been required to source a high proportion of its vehicle purchases from AEC. The link with AEC — self-styled 'Builders of London's Buses', as quoted in publicity — dated back to that company's pre-World War 1 origins as a manufacturer established by LT's predecessor London General. London Transport had continued to collaborate closely with vehicle manufacturers, in furtherance of its policy of developing buses and coaches best suited to London's arduous conditions. As an example, the preselector gearbox had been specified for many London buses since the 1930s, while many provincial buses continued to be fitted with manual transmission. There was also the question of available output from the various manufacturers; for the foreseeable future, Bristol and ECW were likely to be kept busy meeting the requirements of the former Tilling companies now controlled by the BTC, and Richard doubted whether they would be able to cope with substantial orders from London Transport.

The two friends arrived back in Reading at 8pm tired but pleased with their day's travel, in which they had sampled yet more vehicle types in LT's still-varied fleet.

7

North by Northeast

A telephone call from a friend in the Southern Counties Touring Society, advising that the first Central Area RF-class buses had entered service on Thursday 11 September 1952, pitched Richard and John into a day of frenzied planning activity. That coming weekend they were visiting friends who lived in Belsize Park; a telephone call to them elicited the offer of overnight accommodation for both Saturday and Sunday nights, which was accepted gratefully. This would enable Richard and John to fit in a further journey on the Sunday, thus allowing them (hopefully) to travel on a new RF bus as well as riding on further London Transport vehicle types which were due for early withdrawal and which they had not sampled previously.

Travelling with an aristocrat

They travelled up to London on Saturday to visit their friends. After breakfast on Sunday (14 September) they bade farewell for the day to their friends at Belsize Park. Walking up Haverstock Hill on that rather cloudy, fresh morning, they skirted the grounds of the Royal Free Hospital before reaching Hampstead Heath South End Green at around 8.30am. They spent nearly half an hour here, watching the transport activity as well as the sophisticates of Hampstead emerging to buy their Sunday newspapers. Richard and John knew that withdrawal of London Transport's 'B2'-class trolley-buses, allocated to Highgate depot for use on routes

Below: Apart from 37 examples which saw service from 1946 to 1950 on Romford garage's double-deck Green Line routes, London Transport's utility Daimlers were associated exclusively with Merton and Sutton garages. Their superior specification, including Daimler preselector transmission and AEC engine, gave characteristics and performance comparable to London Transport's standard STL class, which allowed them to be mixed on routes shared with other garages. Routes 77 and 77A certainly provided a stern-enough test for any bus on their approximately hour-long journeys from Tooting (77) or Raynes Park (77A) via Clapham Junction and then across Central London to King's Cross. During 1952 Merton's Daimlers shared turns on these 5min-frequency routes with Gillingham Street's STDs and STLs, as well as with Camberwell's and Walworth's RTLs. Brush-bodied Daimler CWA6 D118 (GYL 283) stops in front of St Pancras station, close to journey's end at King's Cross. *G. Rixon*

TROLLEYBUSES AT HAMPSTEAD HEATH

Routes 513/613/615 and 639, which worked from the south side of Hampstead Heath at either South End Green or Parliament Hill Fields, were amongst London Transport's shortest trolleybus routes, with journey times of between 23 and 30 minutes to reach inner London at Holborn or Moorgate.

Above: The 'B' classes, based on Leyland TTB2 chassis, represented the only production batches of short-wheelbase, 60-seat trolleybuses to be bought new by London Transport. Brush-bodied 'B2' No 101 (CGF 101) approaches the terminus at South End Green. *J. C. Gillham*

513/613/615/639, had already started; they were being replaced with 70-seat 'C1'-class vehicles which were themselves being displaced from their home at Fulwell and Isleworth by the arrival of new 'Q1s'. They boarded lightly-loaded 'B2' No 100, which set off at 8.58am, weaving its way along narrow streets and showing why short-wheelbase vehicles had originally been allocated to this group of routes. After travelling through Kentish Town, the 17-year-old Leyland TTB2 passed to the east of Camden Town, down Royal College Street and then along Pancras Road before Richard and John left the Holborn-bound trolleybus outside King's Cross station. The area was a buzz of transport activity, being served by 10 bus and eight trolleybus routes as well as Green

Line route 714. An intruder seen amongst this sea of LT vehicles was a smart, well-loaded, full-fronted, cream-coloured double-decker which passed into Pancras Road bearing route number 203. Richard explained that this was one of independent operator Birch Bros' Willowbrook-bodied Guy Arab IIIs, new in 1951, which had just set off from nearby Judd Street Coach Station on that operator's lengthy route to Rushden. This operated with London Transport's consent, although there was a restriction on the carriage of local passengers between London and Barnet.

Being at King's Cross offered Richard and John the opportunity of a short ride on one of the utility D-class Daimlers. These vehicles were regarded as the aristo-

Right: No 484 (DGY 484) was one of five 'B3'-class trolleybuses with Birmingham Railway Carriage & Wagon Co bodywork built in 1936 to supplement earlier deliveries. Although the chassis design was identical to those earlier builds, a change of nomenclature by Leyland Motors Ltd saw it designated as LPTB60. The characteristic blue 'bullseye' transfer carrying the word 'Trolleybus' on the front panel is missing, leaving a rather plain frontal aspect. *J.C.Gillham*

Left: 'J2B' class No 1001B (EXV 1) was perhaps London Transport's unluckiest trolleybus. The 1938-built AEC 664T had the misfortune to have its original BRCW body destroyed by enemy action at Holloway in October 1940. Subsequently rebodied by Weymann, it then had the further ill luck to suffer damage in another enemy attack, at West Ham Works in July 1944, which destroyed its second body. In 1947 the chassis received its third body, built by East Lancashire Coach Builders, when it also gained the 'B' suffix to its fleetnumber. *J.C.Gillham*

crats amongst London's Utilities, both by their crews and by the Executive. The type's superior specification included Daimler pre-selector transmission and AEC engine, giving them characteristics and performance on a par with London Transport's standard STL class. Nevertheless, in pursuit of its policy of standardisation, London Transport had decided during 1952 that the Daimlers must go, and the first examples had been withdrawn in August.

The friends boarded D127 in York Way, to the east of King's Cross. The empty road of a Sunday morning allowed the driver to show off the Daimler to its best advantage, and it accelerated briskly along Euston Road as the conductress collected their 2d fares. Approaching Euston station, the bus turned left and the sound of its AEC engine echoed down the straight run to Bloomsbury. Shortly afterwards, Southampton Row offered the rather forlorn sight of locked gates at the entrance to the now-redundant Kingsway Subway.

Passing into Kingsway itself, the Daimler pulled up outside Holborn Underground station, where Richard and John alighted. From here they walked eastwards along High Holborn to Chancery Lane. The area's solitude on Sunday morning contrasted with its busy activity during the working week, when seven trolleybus routes terminated here by means of a lengthy loop, either clockwise or anti-clockwise, working from King's Cross to Holborn via Grays Inn Road and Farringdon

Road. Finding the stop for trolleybus route 621 just as 'J1' class No 933 pulled up, they boarded their third near-empty vehicle of the day and sat upstairs at the front. Route 621 followed the clockwise working of the Holborn terminus loop up Grays Inn Road, taking them past King's Cross station again before heading northwards along Caledonian Road. The AEC 664T trolleybus negotiated the busy intersection at Holloway 'Nag's Head' (served by 11 trolleybus routes), turning right into Seven Sisters Road.

By new RF to Golders Green

Richard and John left the North Finchley-bound trolleybus outside Finsbury Park station at 10.14am. After drinking cups of tea bought from a nearby kiosk, the friends walked underneath the low (10ft 6in) railway bridge carrying the main line from King's Cross, and on to Wells Terrace (just north of the station), terminus for routes 210/212 and 233, their information being that RF-class buses had been allocated to the 210. Anxiously they noted the frequent arrival of buses on the busy single-decked routes. Q- and TD-class saloons pulled up at the stand almost every minute, but there was no sign of any RFs. After 20 minutes, just as their eager anticipation was beginning to turn into resigned frustration, brand-new RF292 pulled up at the stand on the 210. Still unused to the concept of passing by the driver to gain access to the saloon, Richard and John boarded by the front entrance and sat on the side-facing bench seat over the nearside front wheel-arch.

After a brief (2min) layover the driver started the engine and the bus pulled away. The conductor got up from the bench seat opposite and collected their 8d fares for Golders Green before passing down the saloon. The underfloor-engined AEC weaved its way around Crouch Hill to Hornsey, making frequent stops on this busy route. At Archway, families intent on a day out on Hampstead Heath boarded. Loaded almost to capacity, the saloon climbed steep Highgate Hill, showing ample reserves of power. After passing the 611 trolleybus terminus in elegant Highgate Village, route 210 continued across the expanse of Hampstead Heath, where many passengers alighted in Spaniards Road to enjoy a walk in the open air on what had now turned into a fine sunny morning. In North End Way RF292 passed Jack Straw's Castle, the highest pub in London, before making a continuous descent to Golders Green and terminating in the spacious Underground station forecourt at 11.26am.

Richard and John had allowed themselves half an hour to see operations of the 12 bus, two trolleybus and five Green Line coach routes — the latter including summer seasonal route 726 (Baker Street–Whipsnade Zoo) — passing through Golders Green. As the time approached 12.00 they headed for the route 102 stop, where the squeal of tightly-adjusted brakes alerted them to the arrival of RT3300. Richard and John boarded and gained front upper-deck seats on this bus, which was bound for High Beach in Epping Forest. The 102 was one of 15 Central Area bus routes which benefited from summer Sunday extensions beyond their usual termini to le Londoners reach beauty spots and attractions. The length

Above: Muswell Hill garage's brand-new Metro-Cammell-bodied AEC Regal IV RF291 (MLL 928) is seen in the company of another at Wells Terrace, Finsbury Park. In compliance with contemporary Metropolitan Police regulations, applicable to all Central Area buses, platform doors were not fitted. *C. Carter*

Above: From March 1952 some of the 6Q6-type former Green Line coaches were temporarily allocated to Muswell Hill garage, following both customer and crew complaints about the condition of single-deck LT-class 'Scooters' on route 210. Q213 (CXX 406) is seen at Archway, heading up Highgate Road. Redundant tram track filled in with asphalt is visible in the foreground at the erstwhile terminus of Kingsway Subway route 35. *J. C. Gillham*

GOLDERS GREEN

Right: The 'prewar' 2RT2/2s, actually built during the early years of the war (in 1939/40), had a long association with both Chelverton Road, Putney, and Putney Bridge garages. The former's RT109 (FXT 284) is seen at Golders Green station on intensive 3/4min-frequency radial route 28, which skirted the perimeter of Central London on its near-hour-long journey to Wandsworth. *M.J.Dryhurst*

Above: In 1937 London Transport took into stock 100 all-Leyland Titan TD4s, modified to some extent to suit LT's requirements. These buses were dubbed the 'Hendon' STDs because of their long association with that garage. One route on which they took up duties in 1937 was the 183, which provided valuable links between Golders Green station and the outer-northwestern suburbs along many stretches of road not served by other bus routes. Rather incredibly, 15 years after their introduction, the 'Hendon' STDs still provided the allocation for route 183 in 1952, as evidenced by a splendid-looking STD78 (DLU 388) on layover in the forecourt of Golders Green station. *J.C.Gillham*

1¼hr journey bisected North East London, passing through Muswell Hill, Palmers Green, Edmonton, Chingford Mount and Chingford.

The bus gained passengers as it progressed, and reached High Beach almost full to capacity. Here Richard and John alighted and, as it was lunchtime, headed for the nearby 'King's Oak' pub. At this time of day the hostelry was naturally very busy, serving cyclists, ramblers and families taking a day out in this 'lung' of London. Fortified with corned-beef sandwiches and shandies, they left the pub at 2.00 and set off to walk to the 'Wake Arms', about 1½ miles distant. The day was now pleasantly warm, and they enjoyed their walk through this remnant of an ancient primæval forest which once stretched from the River Thames to The Wash. After 15 minutes' brisk walk they approached a large white building with London Transport buses parked on its forecourt and knew that they had reached the 'Wake Arms'. The pair spent the next 20 minutes watching an LT inspector supervising the high level of service provided to this terminus in Epping Forest.

At 2.39pm the pair boarded STD139, travelling on this early-postwar standard all-Leyland Titan PD1 for the 10min journey to Epping Town. They spent half an hour here, allowing time for a quick glance into LT's small garage in the High Street, before travelling on to Harlow aboard Bishops Stortford-bound RT1024 on route 396.

Above: A second route worked by Muswell Hill garage to receive a transitory allocation of former Green Line 6Q6 coaches during 1952, in response to dissatisfaction with the LT-class 'Scooters' formerly used, was the 244. Still in Green Line livery but with freshly-painted panels bearing 'LONDON TRANSPORT' fleetnames, 1936-built Q225 (DGX 231) is seen in Powys Road, Southgate, on the 10/15min-frequency route from Winchmore Hill to Muswell Hill. *J. C. Gillham*

Below: One of the smallest Central Area bus garages in terms of both size and allocation was at Church Hill in Loughton. Built by London General shortly after World War 1, in 1952 it had a maximum weekday runout of 41 buses. Its double-deck allocation consisted entirely of all-Leyland Titan PD1s, exemplified by the penultimate STD, STD175 (HLW 104), passing the premises bound for Leytonstone on route 20. Loughton's other double-deck routes were the 38A (Victoria Station–Loughton Station) and 167 (Debden–Ilford), while its complement of former Green Line 10T10 saloons maintained route 254 (Loughton Station–Buckhurst Hill Station). *C. Carter*

HIGH BEACH

Left: In 1952 five Central Area bus routes operated on Summer Sundays only. These included marathon route 35A, which took almost 1¾ hours to travel from Clapham Common, through much of inner South East London and across London Bridge before heading northwards through Shoreditch, Leyton and Walthamstow, to High Beach in Epping Forest; it ran every 12min between noon and 10.30pm. Fortuitously caught by the camera there in 1952 was Camberwell garage's 1951-built RTL1222 (LYF 163). In early 1953 this bus had the misfortune to be destroyed as a result of a fire at Walworth garage. *C. Carter*

Above: High Beach was a popular destination for excursion trips, as evidenced by Private Hire coaches RF7, 25 (LUC 207/25), both allocated to Camberwell garage, photographed on a private charter. The drivers are standing by the removable rear valance panel. The 25 Private Hire RFs, seating 35 passengers, were short-wheelbase, 27ft 6in-long versions of the AEC Regal IV, as compared with 30ft length of the Green Line and bus versions. *C. Carter*

Above: The 'Wake Arms' at Epping Forest provided another example of a public-house forecourt used as a terminus for Central Area bus routes.

On the left of the picture stand Leyton garage's Cravens-bodied RT1485 (KGK 744) and Park Royal-bodied RT2038 (LUC 280) on 12min-frequency Summer Sunday extension of route 38 beyond its usual Royal Forest Hotel terminus. RT1485 has its blinds set for the 1½hr return journey to Victoria station, whilst RT2038 appears to be having some problem attended to by a mechanic.

In the centre is Loughton's STD148 (HLW 77), one of 65 'provincial'-specification all-Leyland Titan PD1s taken into stock by LT in 1946, working route 20 between Leytonstone and Epping Town, on which short-working journeys terminated at the 'Wake Arms'.

On the right, Mann Egerton-bodied Leyland Tiger PS1 TD49 (JXC 242) of Enfield garage has blinds set for a 54min journey on route 242, which skirted the northern perimeter of the Central Area on its way to Potters Bar. *C. Carter*

A (very) New Town

Richard and John had come to Harlow aware that London Transport had introduced its first bus service to Harlow New Town on 20 February 1952. They both wanted to see an embryonic New Town — a postwar phenomenon which was attracting much contemporary comment. They understood from newspaper articles and reports on the wireless that New Towns were intended to re-house people away from overcrowded towns and cities, many districts having suffered bomb damage during World War 2.

Arriving at Harlow Post Office at 3.39pm, the pair crossed the road to the bus stop on the opposite side where at 3.42pm they boarded RT1017 with destination blinds set for Harlow New Town. Having unlimited choice of seats on this completely empty bus, they headed upstairs towards their favourite upper-deck front seat. The conductor collected their fares as the RT turned right off London Road and headed down First Avenue. New semi-detached houses soon came into view, set well back from First Avenue beyond newly-seeded grass verges. An imaginative layout gave ample

space between houses, all of which had decent-sized gardens. Further down First Avenue, completed houses gave way to those still under construction. Although it was a Sunday, bricklayers and hod-carriers, carpenters and tilers were hard at work on this first neighbourhood of Harlow New Town, known as The Stow. Over a period of years, successive neighbourhoods, each with their own shops and services, would be developed, as would industrial estates offering local employment. London Transport would progressively extend bus services to each neighbourhood as it developed, linking them finally with a still-to-be-built 'Town Centre'.

After five minutes' travel the RT pulled up at a deserted crossroads marked 'Road E' and bordered by stacks of bricks. The conductor came upstairs to tell the pair that this was the terminus. He was rather surprised when Richard told him that they wanted to go back to Harlow, instructing them to stay put whilst the bus reversed. This manœuvre completed, the AEC Regent parked beside a temporary LT 'dolly' bus stop.

After an 8min layover RT1017 headed back towards Harlow. Further down First Avenue the bus picked up other passengers. The conductor helped aboard two sets of parents with young children, stacking their pushchairs in the luggage compartment beneath the stairs, and Richard remembered reading that New Towns mostly attracted young families seeking a fresh start in life out in the country. The husbands, both looking smart in their 'demob' suits, were clearly not long out of the Forces.

Cross-country to Waltham Cross

The RT soon regained Old Harlow, where Richard and John alighted opposite the Post Office at 4.00pm. They next wanted to get to Waltham Cross, having planned to do this by reversing their outward journey on routes 396 and 20 to Epping Forest 'Wake Arms', whence they would catch a 242 to Waltham Cross. Making for the stop to catch a southbound 396, due at 4.05pm, they were nonplussed to see an unusual Country Area single-decker approaching on route 393 and displaying the destination 'Hoddesdon'. Richard could hardly believe their luck; this bus was CR4, one of London Transport's

unique batch of rear-engined Leyland Cubs, most of which had been withdrawn in 1949. As it approached, Richard tried frantically to call to mind LT's Country Area map.

'John,' he said, 'we need to take a ride on this one — probably never get another chance. I think if we go to Broxbourne we can then get a 310 down to Waltham Cross. If we're lucky with the connection it'll take about an hour — about as long as it would have taken if we went via "Wake Arms".'

The Leyland had now pulled up at the stop. Richard slid open the door, and the pair mounted the steps of the bus's forward entrance as its driver turned round in his seat to take their fares. They passed down the saloon of the small 20-seat bus, taking the rearmost seats just as the driver engaged gear and the bus began to pull away. The note of its Leyland engine developing power came from underneath this seat, reminding them that this was a rear-engined vehicle. For the next 45 minutes they travelled on this revolutionary (for 1938) bus along narrow Essex lanes and byways,

Below: Consecutively-numbered blocks of new RT buses were often allocated to Country Area garages. In late 1948 Epping garage received 12 Weymann-bodied examples, RT1015-26, all of which were still based there in 1952. RT1017 (JXN 45) is seen at the 'Green Man' terminus at Mulberry Green, Harlow, with blind set for route 396 to Harlow New Town. Confusion caused by the use of the same route number for these spur workings as for trunk route 396, which passed through Harlow *en route* from Epping to Bishops Stortford, led to the New Town journeys' being renumbered 396A from 24 September 1952. *C. Carter*

Left: The CR class, exemplified by CR4 (FXT 110), was another revolutionary 1930s design which emerged as a result of collaboration between London Transport and a chassis manufacturer, in this case Leyland. Based on the latter's Cub chassis, the type featured a vertically-mounted Leyland 4.7-litre engine and gearbox positioned behind the rear axle. This eliminated a long transmission system as well as making the LPTB-built body, of similar style to that fitted to the TF class, suitable for one-man operation. *A. B. Cross*

Below: All-Leyland LPTB70 'K2'-class trolleybus No 1156 (EXV 156) of 1938 waits at Waltham Cross trolleybus terminus in Eleanor Cross Road as the driver of another 'K2', No 1236 (EXV 236), approaches his cab prior to setting off on route 659, thereby leaving a space for 1158 to move onto the twin-wired turning-circle. Waltham Cross trolleybus routes 649, 659 and 679 were lengthy, with journey times in the order of 1 hour to Liverpool Street station, Holborn and Smithfield respectively. *C. Carter*

setting down and collecting occasional passengers in picturesque villages such as Hare Street, Tyler's Cross and Roydon Hamlet. In the fields, harvest (since the war increasingly mechanised with Massey-Harris combine-harvesters) was in full swing. On the Hertfordshire border CR4 became stuck behind a Fordson Major tractor pulling a trailer loaded with sacks of corn, and had to follow it into Broxbourne, where the Cub arrived five minutes behind schedule.

Leaving the bus at Broxbourne station, Richard and John could see an RT approaching down Station Road and dashed to the stop just as RT3500 pulled up on route 310 bound for Enfield. They boarded the five-month-old AEC Regent and went upstairs to find seats. The conductress was kept busy taking fares and supervising the frequent stops on this 10min-frequency route as it headed southwards through Cheshunt; there it met up with Central Area routes 205 and 242 before reaching Waltham Cross, where the pair alighted at 5.07pm. Needing something to drink, they searched in vain for a café — pubs would not be open until 7pm on a Sunday — and eventually settled for 3d ice creams from a mobile Wall's ice-cream salesman parked near

the Eleanor Cross. This had been erected in memory of Edward I's queen, whose body briefly rested here in 1290 on her funeral journey from Lincoln to London.

Finishing their ice creams, the pair walked across to the nearby trolleybus terminus; at 5.32pm they boarded 'K2' No 1182 just before it set off, and took nearside seats just inside the lower deck for their 4min journey along Hertford Road.

Their reason for getting off at this isolated location was in to take a ride on one of the prewar STD-class Leyland Titans. This batch of 100 all-Leyland TD4s was bought in 1937, and they became known affectionately as the 'Hendon' STDs because of their long association with that garage. The friends had learned that from 1 February 1952 a number of these buses had been transferred to Enfield garage, where they had replaced utility Guy Arabs on routes 107/107A (Borehamwood–Ponders End/Enfield Lock). Just as the pair rounded the corner into Ordnance Road, STD72 pulled up on a 107A to Enfield Lock. They boarded the 15-year-old Leyland, which was in smart condition despite its age. It headed off down Ordnance Road, setting down passengers until Richard and John were the last on board as

Below: 'Hendon' STD72 (DLU 382), by then transferred to Enfield garage, lays over outside the entrance to the Royal Small Arms factory at Enfield Lock. *C. Carter*

Above: An 'H1'-class Metro-Cammell-bodied Leyland LPTB70 trolleybus dating from 1938, No 869 (ELB 869) is seen at the Tottenham Court Road terminus of route 629, in front of a bomb-damaged building in Maple Street. The positioning of this terminus, remote from any major traffic objective, exemplifies the handicaps that were put in the way of really successful tram and trolleybus operations, which were proscribed from entering either the City or West End. When proposals to replace trams on the Tottenham Court Road routes with trolleybuses were first put forward, as required by statute, in a Bill before Parliament, London Transport wanted to extend the trolleybus routes from the distant tram terminus at Euston Road down Tottenham Court Road to use a turning circle in Bedford Square — just north of Oxford Street, where many passengers wished to go. Strenuous objections were raised by the Duke of Bedford, the ground landlord, and other residents, resulting in the compromise Maple Street terminus, barely one third of the way down Tottenham Court Road, which came into use with the new trolleybus routes on 8 May 1938. *D. Morris, courtesy T. W. Moore*

the bus pulled up at its terminus at the Royal Small Arms factory. The driver left his cab to talk with the conductor on the platform whilst Richard and John remained seated upstairs. After a 9min layover, at 5.52pm STD72 set off back up Ordnance Road to regain Hertford Road, along which it headed southwards to Ponders End. Turning right into Southbury Road, the Leyland passed its home garage before crossing the A10 Great Cambridge Road and reaching Enfield at 6.14pm, where Richard and John alighted.

Conscious that their friends in Belsize Park would have prepared food for their promised 8pm return, the pair pressed on with their journey. After barely 20 minutes in Enfield — spent mostly in Cecil Road, which offered the spectacle of terminating Country Area routes 310/310A and 313, along with trolleybus route 629 — they boarded 'H1'-class trolleybus No 877, which set off at 6.36pm bound for Tottenham Court Road, an hour distant, on route 629. The trolleybus worked its way southwards through Winchmore Hill and Palmers Green to Wood Green, where it passed the entrance to its home depot. From here onwards the scale of London

Transport trolleybus operation truly became apparent, as route 629 ran under wires also used by several other routes and 877 was passed by an almost continuous procession of oncoming trolleybuses. At Manor House the 629 turned right into Seven Sisters Road, passing Finsbury Park before crossing Holloway Road at the 'Nag's Head'. Having reached Camden Town, Richard and John alighted and crossed over the High Street. After a few minutes they saw 'B2'-class trolleybus No 124 approaching on route 639, and boarded as 124's driver switched on its internal lights. The 60-seat Leyland set off in the gathering twilight along Chalk Farm Road before climbing to Hampstead Heath South End Green, whence the pair had set out nearly 11 hours earlier.

Walking back to their friends' house in Belsize Park, Richard and John reflected on their day's travel as well as the other journeys that they had made around London that year. They both agreed that they had indeed been privileged to have seen for themselves — as well as travelled upon — many examples of the fascinating variety of buses, trams and trolleybuses that operated in London during 1952.

105

Journey schedule

Sunday 14 September 1952

Terminus	Dep/Arr	Route No	Vehicle	Allocation	Fare
Hampstead Heath (South End Green)	8.58am	513	'B2' 100	HT	5d
King's Cross	9.13am				
King's Cross (York Way)	9.32am	77A	D127	AL	2d
Kingsway (Holborn LT Station)	9.40am				
Holborn (Chancery Lane)	9.54am	621	'J1' 933	FY	5d
Finsbury Park (LT Station)	10.14am				
Finsbury Park (Wells Terrace)	10.54am	210	RF292	MH	8d
Golders Green (LT Station)	11.26am				
Golders Green (LT Station)	12.00pm	102	RT3300	AD	1/11d
High Beach	1.16pm				
Epping Forest (Wake Arms)	2.39pm	20	STD139	L	5d
Epping Town (High Street)	2.49pm				
Epping Town (High Street)	3.21pm	396	RT1024	EP	9d
Harlow (Post Office)	3.39pm				
Harlow (Post Office)	3.42pm	396	RT1017	EP	2d
Harlow New Town (Road 'E')	3.47pm				
Harlow New Town (Road 'E')	3.55pm	396	RT1017	EP	2d
Harlow (Post Office)	4.00pm				
Harlow (Post Office)	4.05pm	393	CR4	EP	1/3d
Broxbourne (Station Road)	4.49pm				
Broxbourne (Station Road)	4.50pm	310	RT3500	HG	8d
Waltham Cross	5.07pm				
Waltham Cross	5.32pm	649	'K2' 1182	EM	5d
(Hertford Road)	5.36pm				
Ordnance Road	5.37pm	107A	STD72	E	2d
Enfield Lock (RSA Factory)	5.43pm				
Enfield Lock (RSA Factory)	5.52pm	107A	STD72	E	6d
Enfield Town (Church Street)	6.14pm				
Enfield Town (Cecil Road)	6.36pm	629	'H1' 877	WN	1/-
Camden Town (High Street)	7.25pm				
Camden Town (High Street)	7.34pm	639	'B2' 124	HT	3d
Hampstead Heath (South End Green)	7.42pm				

8

Fascinating Facets

DOUBLE-DECK FRONT DESTINATION DISPLAYS

During 1952 London Transport double-deck buses could be seen with two principal forms of front destination display.

Right: Putney Bridge garage's RTW417 (LLU 567) seen at Putney Heath 'Green Man' displays the restricted style of front destination display first introduced in 1941, principally to comply with wartime blackout regulations — although it did save blind linen too. In 1947 this design was modified by offsetting the route number and thereby allowing the intermediate points to be used for workings in either direction. *Author's collection*

Left: Bus route 45 replaced tram route 34 on 1 October 1950, being extended from the latter's Battersea Bridge terminus to South Kensington station, where this view of RTL1094 (LUC 287) was taken in July 1952. A comprehensive five-line intermediate display sits above a final destination display in which the suffix 'ONLY' was intended to indicate a short working — route 45 in its entirety ran to Farringdon Street. This qualification confused some passengers, who thought that it meant that the bus operated non-stop. Under the canopy may be seen another route-number display, as well as a removable board highlighting the route's links to Battersea Park Pleasure Gardens. Also clearly visible on the front nearside are Clapham garage's stencil and running number (CA12). *G.H.F. Atkins*

Diversions

London Transport's services were subject to a number of temporary disruptions and diversions in 1952. Many such instances were caused by 'routine' roadworks, as well as cable- and sewer-laying. In addition, the removal of redundant tramway tracks caused route diversions in Balham, Kennington, Lambeth and Lewisham. Other annual disruptions included the New Year's Eve celebrations, centred on the Eros statue in Piccadilly Circus, and the University Boat Race on Saturday 29 March, during which Hammersmith Bridge was closed. Just seven years after the cessation of hostilities, memories of World War 2 were still very fresh, and as well as the nation's annual Remembrance Day on Sunday 9 November, there were 10 other occasions during the year when services were held at the Cenotaph, requiring the closure of Whitehall and thus necessitating the diversion of bus and Green Line coach routes.

The death of HM King George VI on 6 February at Balmoral plunged the nation into mourning. Following the return of the Royal coffin by train to London on Monday 11 February, the cortège's progress from King's Cross station to Westminster Hall necessitated extensive route diversions throughout Central London. During the late King's lying-in-state over the next three days, crowds of mourners from all over the country and abroad, wishing to pay their respects, became so large that bus and Green Line coach routes had to be diverted away from Millbank and Lambeth Bridge. On Friday 15 February the funeral procession caused extensive diversion of routes in Central London as the cortège moved in late morning from Westminster Hall to Paddington station whence the Royal Train carried the coffin and mourners to Windsor. Country Bus and Green Line coach routes were disrupted in the Royal Borough until after the funeral service at St George's Chapel. LT staff were asked to respect the national two minutes' silence at 2.00pm: drivers were instructed to stop their vehicles, switch off engines and, where possible, dismount from cabs and stand to attention beside their buses. The subsequent Royal Proclamation of Coronation of the late King's heir and successor, the future Queen Elizabeth II, caused bus and coach routes serving Trafalgar Square to be disrupted during the morning of Saturday 7 June.

ADVERSE WEATHER

London Transport had to endeavour to maintain services in all weather conditions. One persistent winter problem was 'smog', when fog mixed with chimney and factory smoke to form an almost impenetrable 'pea souper'. Ice and snow presented difficulties too, as evidenced by this shot of former Leyton Corporation 'E/3'-class tramcar No 186 at Archway terminus at the bottom of Highgate Hill, during an unexpectedly-late heavy snowfall on 29 March 1952. *J. C. Gillham*

Above: Hammersmith Bridge was closed for repairs from 16 July to 23 August 1952. Routes 9 (Mortlake to Liverpool Street [weekdays] or Becontree Heath [Sundays]), 72 (Esher–East Acton) and 73 (Stoke Newington–Richmond) were split to terminate at either end of the bridge, with through passengers having to walk across to catch a connecting bus. Route 33 (Hammersmith–Hounslow) was diverted via Chiswick Bridge, whilst Green Line routes 714, 715, 716 and 717 were diverted via Putney Bridge. On Sundays Barking shared in the operation of route 9, and that garage's RTL301 (KGU 259) is seen at the temporary terminus in Hammersmith Bridge Road, ready to set out for Becontree Heath, 1½ hours distant. *C. Carter*

FESTIVAL GARDENS SERVICES

The 1951 Festival of Britain heralded the beginning of national emergence from the drab, grey 'austerity' era that continued long after the end of World War 2. One attraction which continued in subsequent years was the Festival Gardens at Battersea Park, incorporating a Fun Fair with such features as the Rotor Ride, Tree Walk and Water Splash. In 1952 London Transport re-introduced special bus routes A and B, and these operated from 24 May to 18 October. The two routes shuttled from about midday until late evening between the Underground stations at South Kensington (A) or Sloane Square (B) and the Festival Gardens. Well-loaded RTL400 (KGU 487) of Stockwell garage is shown discharging passengers, who would have paid 3d for the ride from Sloane Square station, at Queenstown Road, just south of Chelsea Bridge. *C. Carter*

PRIVATE HIRE

Under the terms of the 1933 Act, London Transport had been prevented from operating private-hire journeys further than 10 miles beyond the boundary of the London Passenger Transport Area (5 miles in Kent). Coastal resorts were thus 'out of bounds' to London Transport, but this all changed when the British Transport Commission issued a directive authorising LT to operate private hires to any point within a 100-mile radius of 55 Broadway, with effect from 30 May 1950.

Above: Fifteen RFW-class Eastern Coach Works-bodied AEC Regal IV 'long-distance' coaches, built to the (then) recently-relaxed dimensions of 8ft width and 30ft length, joined LT's fleet in 1951 — representing a rare coming together of the state-owned bodybuilder and state-owned London Transport. RFW9 (LUC 384) powers south along the A23 Purley Way, most likely heading for a South Coast destination such as Brighton. *Aviation & Transport Photographs, courtesy R. Marshall*

Right: London Transport also made extensive use of double-deck buses for private-hire work, as exemplified by Chelverton Road, Putney, garage's RT91 (FXT 266) also seen heading southwards along the Purley Way.
The concern expressed by London's coach operators at what they perceived as a threat posed to their business by LT's newly-extended private-hire area was probably justified, since the sight of convoys of LT double-deckers heading for coastal resorts became quite usual at summer weekends. *Aviation & Transport Photographs, courtesy R. Marshall*

Left: At the beginning of 1952 most Central Area (red) bus routes still had separately-priced tickets produced by the Bell Punch Co, listing geographically all the fare stages along a route — or routes, if a crew worked on more than one during a shift. This 6½d ticket included stages for both trunk route 15 (Kew Gardens–East Ham) and irregular route 100 (Barking–Beckton Gas Works), which were interworked from Upton Park garage. *G. Page collection*

Fares and tickets

At the start of 1952 the fares on LT's buses, trams and trolleybuses remained the same as those introduced on 1 October 1950. That fare revision had had most effect on the trams and trolleybuses, and had eliminated the system of transfer tickets and workman's returns which had previously existed within the LCC area, along with other non-standard fares inherited from the former Company and municipal tramway operations. A cheap (6d) midday fare within the LCC area (previously 4d), and between Norbury and Purley on trams, trolleybuses and those bus routes which paralleled them, was still available. From October 1950, to compensate for the withdrawal of workman's returns on trams and trolleybuses, on most Central and Country Area services LT had introduced early-morning single fares of 2d (up to 10 miles), rising to 6d for the longest Country Area journeys. These applied on weekdays only.

Fares revision 2 March 1952

This was a milestone for London fares and tickets. The British Transport Commission (Passenger) Charges Scheme 1952 provided for revised fares on all London Transport services and the railways of the Railway Executive throughout the country. The revised fares came into operation for London on 2 March 1952.

Right: New tram-replacement bus routes introduced after October 1950 used tickets produced in London Transport's own printing works at Effra Road, Brixton. These were numerical stage tickets but showed route numbers grouped for each garage. This 8d ticket was for use by Rye Lane (RL) garage on routes 69, 149, 178, 179 and 285. *G. Page collection*

Above: TIMs — machines issuing plain-paper tickets — were in use at Camberwell, Cricklewood and Victoria (Gillingham Street) Central Area bus garages, as well as at Fulwell and Isleworth trolleybus depots. This 5d ticket was issued by a Gillingham Street conductor on route 77. There were also spasmodic appearances of experimental Gibson paper-ticket-issuing machines — later developed by LT to become the standard method of ticket issue on all bus and trolleybus services. *G. Page collection*

Left: All tram and trolleybus tickets were printed at Effra Road. Most routes used one of two separate sets of numbered stage tickets, headed 'A' or 'B', each with a different array of stages. The 'A' example, illustrated, covered 27 stages (including reverse side). *G. Page collection*

Left: A few experimental Ultimate machines were in use at Muswell Hill garage. Tickets for these machines were pre-printed with fare values, whilst the issuing machine printed the fare stage. The Ultimate was later developed by LT as the standard machine for one-man-operated buses. *G. Page collection*

Right: Kingsway Subway tram routes 33 and 35 had their own separate numerical set of tickets which carried numbers in both the Northern and Southern area stage systems. *G. Page collection*

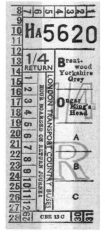

Ordinary fares were based on a scale of 1½d a mile, fractions of 1d being charged as 1d. The minimum 1½d adult fare rose to 2d, 3d unchanged, 4d to 5d, 5d to 6d, 6½d to 8d, 8d to 9d, 9d to 11d, 10d to 1s 0d, 11½d to 1s 2d, and so on. The early-morning single-fare scale increased to a minimum of 3d, rising to 9d for the longest Country Bus journey. Children's fares became exactly one half of the adult fare on all services. In an attempt to eliminate historical fare anomalies and obtain a distance of one mile for the new minimum single fare of 2d, some existing fare stages were withdrawn and a number of new ones introduced. Subsequent to the general revision, on 30 March, early-morning single fares became available for all journeys scheduled to finish at or before 8.00am.

Fares revision 31 August 1952

The introduction of additional fare stages in the March revision had caused much controversy and resentment among the travelling public. Some increased fares had 'double jumped' in the new scale; for example, some 1½d fares had become 3d, some 3d fares 5d, and so on. Under some Government pressure — reputedly directed by Prime Minister Winston Churchill — London

Above: Six-day (12-journey) weekly tickets, printed by Bell Punch, were available in the northern half of the Country Area. This was a legacy of operations by LT's predecessors in much of that territory prior to the 1933 Act — National Omnibus & Transport Co and Amersham & District. As evidenced by this 6/9d example valid until 30 August 1952 between Luton and Harpenden 'George', these were separately-priced blank tickets upon which journey limits were entered manually at garage or enquiry office. An exception was to be found at Uxbridge, where a range of tickets with printed journeys was stocked at the LT station. *G. Page collection*

Transport was forced to revert to the fare stages in operation prior to 2 March, except for those introduced to enable certain fares to be extended for passengers' benefit. Fares on the general scale introduced on 2 March were then re-calculated to the original stages. One exception was the former 1½d fare between Westminster and Southampton Row (tram routes 33/35); this remained at 3d (bus routes 171/172) because of the lengthened route followed by the buses, due to the closure of the Kingsway Subway. The range of numerical tickets continued in use as before, but the opportunity was taken to introduce a separate 3d morning ticket. At this time, fare-stage labels were applied to bus stops for the first time.

In summary, 1952 saw the Executive's efforts to contain costs and increase revenue frustrated to some extent by Government meddling in its affairs. Operationally, the further simplification of the fare structure, started in 1950, was a precursor to the introduction of ticket mechanisation, which began in earnest in 1953.

For the enthusiast and ticket collector, the informative and colourful Green Line tickets offered some compensation for the loss of the huge variety of geographical tickets formerly issued on Central Area buses.

Left: Green Line issued stage single and return tickets printed by the Bell Punch Co. There were 16 different series of single tickets in use for garages operating Green Line services, with values ranging from 1d to 4/4d — the lowest values being used to make up children's or long-distance fares. Tickets bore geographical (but un-numbered) fare stages. Those for use by Amersham and Windsor garages were the largest, each bearing stages for three routes. The Windsor garage ticket illustrated lists (including on the reverse side) fare stages for routes 704 (Windsor–Tunbridge Wells), 705 (Windsor–Sevenoaks) and 718 (Windsor–Epping). *G. Page collection*

Right: Evidence that LT's monopoly position did not necessarily give passengers the best fares deal was provided by the fact that by 1952 the only Green Line day-return fares available were over common sections of route served by independent operators — Birch Bros and City Coach Co — which themselves offered return fares. This 5/6d return fare was issued on route 716 between London and Hitchin — between which points passengers could also travel on Birch Bros route 203. *G. Page collection*

Above: LT's acquisition of Eastern National's Grays-area routes (on 30 September 1951) introduced five-day (10-journey) Workman's weekly tickets to the Country Bus & Coach Department. The unissued 2/5d five-day example illustrated was available on route 349 to Thames Haven — at only nine miles from Southend the most easterly point ever reached by an LT bus route — as well as on routes 367 and 368 to the BATA shoe factory at East Tilbury. On both five-and six-day weekly tickets the passenger was required to sign the reverse side and write his/her address on it. *G. Page collection*

Left: A representative Central Area 2½d 26-stage Bell Punch ticket of the style introduced in March 1952. These were quickly dubbed 'Deaf & Dumb' tickets because the named fare stages on previous issues had been replaced simply by fare-stage numbers. *G. Page collection*

Above: Luggage or other bulky items not exceeding 28lb in weight could be carried on the front platform of trams beside the motorman for 2d — a price which had held good since horse-tram days. Passengers reclaimed an item by presenting a ticket with an identical number to the sticker placed on the item. *G. Page collection*

Above: Special souvenir tickets were printed at Effra Road for general use throughout Last Tram Week. There were 10 different tickets in the set, ranging from 1d to 11d and including 1½d and 2½d child tickets. The reverse sides of the tickets shown featured pioneer George Francis Train's horse trams — which started work on London's first tramway on 23 March 1861 — as well as an 'E/3' car. *G. Page collection*

Left: A completely new series of geographical-stage tickets was introduced on the Green Line network coincident with the fares revision of 2 March 1952. To acquaint conductors with forthcoming ticket mechanisation, the tickets also carried stage numbers for the first time, the numbering being so arranged that the Central London point (or terminus) was 35. The general range in use ran from 1d to 4/6d; printed on both sides, this 1/11d ticket covered all stages for East London Green Line routes 721, 722, 723 and 723A. *G. Page collection*

Left: Whilst Hammersmith Bridge was closed for repairs between 16 July and 23 August 1952, passengers with through tickets on bus routes 9, 72 and 73 were required to walk across the bridge to catch an onward-connecting journey. To remove opportunities for fraudulent travel using the recently-introduced numerical-stage trickets, LT reintroduced special geographical tickets on these routes only. On Sundays, when route 9 worked a lengthy extension to Becontree Heath, some buses cross-worked to run journeys on irregularly-scheduled route 23C (Becontree–Creekmouth Power Station), and a set of geographical tickets headed '9S/23C' was specially printed for such use. *G. Page collection*

Above: Weekly six-day (12-journey) tickets continued to be available on the Green Line network for journeys to a Central London point. These were printed using numerical stages, with the exception of the frequent East London routes, which used printed geographical tickets, as exemplified by this 18/- ticket issued for use on route 722. *G. Page collection*

Right: On 1 October 1952 a charge to passengers was introduced on the coach services operated on BEA's behalf by LT from Kensington Air Station to London (Heath Row) and Northolt airports; these had previously been provided on a complementary basis. Tickets, which were date-punched on issue, were sold by non-travelling conductors stationed at each terminus. Illustrated is a green-coloured 5/- adult ticket issued from London Airport. *G. Page collection*

SUPPORT SERVICES

London Transport ran about 500 vehicles in support of the Executive's passenger transport operations.

Above: Splendid-looking Karrier breakdown wagon No 176K, running on trade plates 137 GC, originated with London County Council Tramways. It is seen in the Old Kent Road on 19 April 1952 when allocated to New Cross tram depot. The massive front bumper-bar was used for pushing disabled trams, as illustrated in Chapter 2.
J. C. Gillham

Left: London Transport had provided mobile canteen facilities at many principal termini since 1937. Converted buses were used from inception until gradually displaced from 1947 onwards by purpose-built articulated trailer units pulled by Bedford tractor units. AEC Regent ST922 (GJ 2098), new to Thomas Tilling Ltd in 1930, was the last former bus to be commissioned as a mobile canteen, on 8 April 1947. Renumbered 693J, it is seen in use on 27 July 1952 at Windmill Lane, off Greenford Broadway. Displaced from canteen duties in November 1954, 693J languished for many years at Rush Green Motors' premises in Hertfordshire before being rescued for preservation by Prince Marshall in 1966, ultimately being restored to its former glory as ST922 and taking once more to the streets of London. *J. C. Gillham*

Above: Amersham garage's RLH4 (KYY 504), working route 336, just clears the low railway bridge at Amersham Common used by both British Railways and LT's Metropolitan Line. *J. C. Gillham*

Left: On a crowded lowbridge bus, travelling upstairs — wedged tightly on a bench seat between fellow passengers — tested both manners and tolerance. The gentleman 'lighting up' on utility Daimler D130 demonstrates a further hazard of top-deck travel in 1952 — involuntary passive smoking. *A. B. Cross*

Right: Merton garage's Duple-bodied Daimler CWA6 D6 (GXE 583) seen towards the very end of its London Transport life, at South Wimbledon Station terminus in Milner Road on 27 November 1952. This bus was amongst those bought by dealer W. North of Leeds in December 1952 and exported to South Western Omnibus Co of Colombo, Ceylon. *J. C. Gillham*

Lowbridge routes

An LT *Traffic Circular* issued in 1952, listing 370 bridges under which double-deck buses should not be driven, might give the impression that LT's operating area was riddled with low bridges. Whilst some dictated the use of single-deck buses, the great majority were avoided by bus routes. In 1952 London Transport operated just eight bus routes, listed in Appendix 8, which necessitated the use of 13ft4in-high lowbridge buses, referred to in the same *Traffic Circular* as 'low loader type'. As Appendix 8 shows, at the beginning of 1952 LT's lowbridge routes were worked by some of its oldest double-deck buses — 1930 ST-class AEC Regents, along with mid-1930s STLs — as well as 10 utility-bodied Daimlers and the first 20 RLH-class AEC Regent IIIs, delivered in 1950. Between October and December 1952, LT took into stock a further 56 RLH-class lowbridge buses, and by the year's end these displaced from passenger service all prewar and utility lowbridge buses. The increased size of LT's lowbridge fleet, which now comprised 76 RLH-class vehicles, exceeded the required allocation to garages operating lowbridge routes, resulting in some RLH buses' being allocated to Country Area routes with no height restrictions.

Above: A passenger exercises the perceived right of all Londoners to hop on or off a bus whenever it is held up by traffic. STL1978 (BXW 938) was a 1937 AEC Regent whose original highbridge body was replaced by one of 20 specially-authorised Chiswick-built lowbridge bodies in 1942. The bus is seen pulling out of Mason's Avenue onto the bridge near Harrow & Wealdstone station. STL1978 was withdrawn in December 1952, subsequently passing to Basil Williams' Hants & Sussex fleet. The television shop to the left of the picture would certainly have been experiencing a boom, considering that the number of TV licences held throughout the country doubled from $^3/_4$ million in 1951 to $1^1/_2$ million in 1952. *Ian Allan Library*

Right: Veteran 48-seat Short Bros-bodied AEC Regent ST162 (GF 7218), which started life with National Omnibus & Transport Co Ltd in 1930, is seen at Rayners Lane in 1952, when allocated to Harrow Weald garage for route 230. This and sister vehicle ST141 were withdrawn in October 1952, being displaced by two STL19s transferred from Godstone garage, which latter were themselves withdrawn two months later when Harrow Weald garage received its full complement of new RLH buses. *C. Carter*

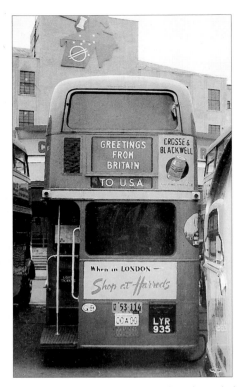

The North American tour buses

On 8 March 1952 three London Transport double-deck buses embarked on the liner *Parthia* for New York. They were sponsored by the British Travel & Holidays Association to tour the USA and Canada in connection with that organisation's 'Come to Britain' campaign. The buses concerned — Park Royal-bodied AEC Regents RT2775/6 (LYR 826/7) and Weymann-bodied Leyland Titan RTL1307 (LYR 935) — were chosen to be representative of LT's principal suppliers. Accompanied by LT crews and mechanics with support vehicles, the three buses completed a 12,000-mile tour of North America. RT2776 was selected to give rides to the American populace, for which it received a number of modifications to meet American conditions and regulations. These included an enhanced ventilation system, pilot-injection engine, shock absorbers on the front axle, large-section tyres, more powerful headlights and a higher rear-axle ratio. RT2775 was equipped as a mobile exhibition unit, whilst RTL1307 was fitted out as both a mobile workshop and the crew's quarters.

The tour created much interest and generated much goodwill, although the buses nevertheless attracted what might be termed 'constructive criticism'; one American correspondent, who rode on RT2776 in Philadelphia, wrote in *Buses Illustrated* No 11 (published in July 1952):

'Many Americans like the double-decker buses, except for the fact that the motors are in front. We realize your axle and weight restrictions, but why cut down capacity? If the engine were mounted under the rear steps (where the conductor stands) and the driver placed at the extreme

Above: The three American Tour buses acquired 'GB' plates, which remained on the vehicles when they returned to ordinary duties in London. RTL1307 displays its 'GB' plate beside assorted American plates; the marker lights and extra ventilation panel fitted for the tour are also visible. *G.W.Morant*

TUNNEL STLs

In 1937 London Transport took delivery of 40 STL-class AEC Regents fitted with modified Chiswick-built highbridge bodies incorporating inward-sloping upper-deck pillars and arched roofs designed to give adequate clearance from the tight, tubular profile of the Blackwall Tunnel. Roadworks in 1951 to replace granite setts in the tunnel's roadway and reduce its camber meant that normal-profile double-deckers could thereafter pass through. However, the 'Tunnel STLs', allocated to Athol Street garage, continued in use throughout 1952, as evidenced by STL1844 (DLU 213), emerging from the tunnel's southern portal while working route 108 (Bromley-by-Bow–Crystal Palace). The narrow tunnel roadway, which carried traffic in both directions, required all buses working through the tunnel, as well as those on route 82 through the Rotherhithe Tunnel, to be fitted with reinforced tyres to withstand scuffing the kerb. *J.C.Gillham*

front, next to a front entrance, it would eliminate the necessity, and thereby the expense, of two men per bus.' (These words doubtless represent heresy to many London Transport enthusiasts who are reading this book!)

The buses returned to by met by the Rt Hon A. T. Lennox-Boyd MP, the Minister of Transport, at an official welcoming ceremony at Horse Guards Parade on 20 August 1952.

Christmas Day

Central Road Services provided services on 137 bus and 52 trolleybus routes on Christmas Day 1952. In general, services operated between 7.30am and 4.00pm, although selected routes featured some early-morning journeys. The highest frequencies were provided by route 16 between Cricklewood and Victoria and trolleybus route 691 between Barkingside and Ilford, both of which operated every three minutes. The average route frequency was around 10 minutes, although the outer sections of routes 20 (Loughton–Epping Town) and 87 (Rainham War Memorial–White Post Corner) were restricted to a 30min headway. Eighteen bus routes continued operating after 4.00pm to provide a service until around 10.30pm. Night bus and trolleybus routes operated on the night of 24/25 December but were suspended for the night of 25/26 December.

The Country Bus & Coach Department operated special services on 66 bus routes as well as on all Green Line coach routes. Bus routes with a service on Christmas Day included the lengthy 301 (Watford Junction–Aylesbury) and 408 (Croydon–Guildford).

Above: Had this working been photographed a year earlier, one of Sutton garage's 'relaxed austerity' Daimlers would have filled the frame; RTLs started to displace the Daimlers from October 1952. One such was brand-new RTL1372 (MXX 95), seen at Morden station on Christmas Day, when route 156 ran every 7½min to North Cheam, with alternate journeys extended via Sutton to complete a circular working back to Morden. *A. B. Cross*

DISPOSALS

London Transport's disposal of serviceable vehicles in 1952 occurred during a period when delivery of new vehicles from manufacturers was very extended. This created a demand for secondhand buses from domestic operators anxious to update their fleets. The market in used buses abroad was also brisk, stimulated in some cases by international aid packages aimed at restoring economies ravaged by war. Some representative disposals are illustrated. During the year other ex-LT utility Guy Arabs were sold to operators in the Canary Islands, where they were rebodied with locally-built single-deck bodies. Yet others were sold on to Africa, 11 going to Trans-Rhodes Services of Salisbury, Rhodesia (another operator to rebody them as single-deckers) and three being despatched to Kenya Bus Service of Nairobi.

Two operators in Ceylon — Colombo Omnibus Co and South Western Omnibus Co — also received substantial numbers of utility Guy Arabs, with the latter also taking some of LT's first Daimler Utility disposals towards the end of the year, these being lowbridge examples. Several 9T9-variant T-class AEC Regals were also exported, a couple being traced to Trans-Rhodes Services. Two 1941-built 'unfrozen' STL-class AEC Regents, meanwhile, were exported to Baghdad, Iraq.

Above: Between 1949 and 1951 London Transport's most modern tramcars, the 90 remaining 1930/1-built 'Felthams', were sold for further service to Leeds City Transport. Former LT No 2095 is seen at Leeds' very rural Temple Newsam terminus in April 1952, bearing fleetnumber 543. *G.W.Morant*

Above: Weymann-bodied Guy Arab I G36 (GLF 686) was the forerunner of many London Transport buses sold for further service in Yugoslavia. Renumbered 91 and re-registered GXO 238, the bus is seen on 21 August 1952 in the ownership of Autoprevos, departing Basarska market place in Sarajevo bound for Ilidze, 7 miles distant, on a route formerly worked by a steam tram. Already with several window glasses missing and damage to body panels, the bus still displays its LT fleetnumber on its rear dome as evidence of its erstwhile allocation to Upton Park, where fleetnumbers were thus applied to facilitate identification from that garage's overhead fuel gantry. Sarajevo tram No 53, pulling a trailer, heads into the market place. *J.C.Gillham*

Right: Fifty surplus London Transport Guy Arabs were sold to the Scottish Omnibuses group. Park Royal-bodied Guy Arab II G344 (HGC 123), numbered E28 in the ownership of Scottish Omnibuses Ltd displays the traditional SMT motif at St Andrew Square, Edinburgh, in 1952. Many of the former LT Guy Arabs sold to Scottish Omnibuses were subsequently rebodied or extensively rebuilt to give many further years of service; E28 was withdrawn in 1953 to become one of nine such vehicles which re-emerged in 1954 as single-deck buses for use by Highland Omnibuses and Scottish Omnibuses. Scottish Omnibuses and its predecessor SMT had much prior experience in rebuilding vehicles; AEC Regent BB8 (FS 5566), seen at the rear, was rebuilt from a 1933 AEC Regal chassis, receiving a lowbridge Alexander body in 1944. *R. Grieves collection*

Below: Sixty former London Transport Guy Arab IIs were sold to Edinburgh Corporation Transport. Their utility bodies were scrapped and the chassis extensively rebuilt, receiving new full-front bodywork designed by Duple but mostly built by associate bodybuilder Nudd Bros & Lockyer at Kegworth, Leicestershire. The resultant handsome and modern product is represented by Edinburgh Corporation No 336 (JWS 616); passing along Princes Street beside a typical mid-1930s Edinburgh tram built in the Corporation's own Shrubhill Works, it is quite unrecognisable as the former LT No G258 (GYL 397). *R. Grieves collection*

Appendix 1
Tramcars owned by London Transport Executive at 1 January 1952

Class	Years built	Original ownership	Quantity	
E/1 *	1907-30	London County Council	99	
	1927/8	Croydon Corporation	20	
	1927/8	East Ham Corporation	20	
	1926-32	Walthamstow Corporation	16	
	1929-31	West Ham Corporation	30	
				185
E/3 §	1930/1	London County Council	91	
	1930/1	Leyton Corporation	50	
				141
HR/2 §	1930	London County Council	52	
				52
TOTAL				378

* Some 'E/1' cars reconditioned 1935/6   § One 'E/3' and 15 'HR/2' cars equipped for conduit operation only

Appendix 2
Trolleybuses owned by London Transport Executive in 1952

Class(es)	Years built	Quantity 1 January 1952	Quantity 31 December 1952
A1/A2	1931	10	–
X1/X2/X3	1933/4	3	3
B1/B2/B3	1935/6	76	76
C1/C2/C3	1935-7	251	251
D1/D2/D3	1936/7	152	152
E1/E2/E3	1937	100	100
F1	1937	100	100
H1	1938	147	147
J1/J2/J3	1938	148	148
K1/K2/K3	1938-40	325	325
L1/L2/L3	1938-40	172	172
X4/X5/X6/X7	1937-40	4	4
M1	1939/40	25	25
N1/N2	1939/40	115	115
P1	1941	25	25
SA1/SA2/SA3	1941-3	43	43
Q1	1948-52	77	125
TOTAL		1773	1811

Appendix 3
Motor buses owned by London Transport Executive in 1952

Class	Years built	Quantity 1 January 1952	Quantity 31 December 1952
Double-deck			
ST	1930	8	8
STL	1932-46	941	927
STD	1937-46	176	176
B	1942-5	29	27
G *	1942-6	284	120
D	1944-6	281	236
RT	1939-52	3570	3993
RTL	1948-52	1281	1389
RTW	1949/50	500	500
RTC	1949	1	1
SRT	1949	160	160
RLH	1950-2	20	76
TOTAL DOUBLE-DECK		7251	7613

Single-deck			
T	1929-48	440	392
LT	1931/2	98	88
Q	1935/6	231	215
C	1935/6	72	70
LTC	1937/8	24	23
CR	1939	29	20
TF	1939	76	71
TD	1946-8	131	131
RF	1951/2	110	425
RFW	1951	15	15
TOTAL SINGLE-DECK		1226	1450
GRAND TOTAL		8477	9063

* G436 new 1949

Appendix 4
Central Road Services tramway depots — allocation to routes at 1 January 1952

Depot	Number of trams scheduled			Routes operated
	M-F	Sat	Sun	
Abbey Wood	52	55	24	36 38 44 46 46EX
Highgate *	14	13	11	33 35§
New Cross	218	225	122	5$ 35 36 38 40 46 52 54 72 72EX 74
Norwood	39	39	18	33 48 78
TOTALS	323	332	175	

* Shared premises with HT (Highgate) trolleybus depot

§ Night service also operated Sunday-Friday nights

$ Night service only, Sunday-Friday nights

Appendix 5
Central Road Services trolleybus depots — allocation to routes at 1 January 1952

Code	Depot	Number of trolleybuses scheduled			Routes operated
		M-F	Sat	Sun	
BW	Bow	98	95	56	661 663 695
BX	Bexley	77	69	47	696 698
CE	Colindale	39	36	28	645 660 664 666
CN	Carshalton	29	29	21	654
CT	Clapton	74	51	33	555 581 677
EM	Edmonton	116	119	95	627 649 659 679
FW	Fulwell	85	90	69	601 602 603 604 605 667
FY	Finchley	79	79	72	521 609 621 645 660 664 666
HB	Hammersmith	69	73	53	626 628 630*
HL	Hanwell	109	105	70	607 655
HT§	Highgate	153	160	91	513* 517 611 613* 615 617 627 639 653
ID	Ilford	39	39	28	691 693 695
IH	Isleworth	27	24	17	657
LB	Lea Bridge	25	19	10	581
PR	Poplar	85	66	44	565 567 569 665*
SE	Stonebridge	83	73	51	645 660 662 664 666
SF	Stamford Hill	66	64	33	543* 643* 647 649 649A 683
WH	West Ham	152	138	80	565 567 569 665 669 685 687 689 690 697 699
WN	Wood Green	98	96	54	623 625 627 629 641
WW	Walthamstow	100	92	68	557 623 625 685 697 699
TOTALS		1603	1517	1020	

* Night service also operated Sunday-Friday nights

§ Shared premises with Highgate tram depot until 6 April 1952

Appendix 6
Central Road Services bus garages — scheduled allocation to routes at 6 July 1952 (immediately following final tramway withdrawal)

Code	Garage	Bus types	Number of buses scheduled			Routes operated[1,2]
			M-F	Sat	Sun	
A	Sutton	STL, D, LT	128	124	106	80 80A 93 115 151 156 164 164A 213
AB	Twickenham	RT, SRT	49	54	44	27 27A 27B 71 90 90B 111
AC	Willesden	RT, RTW	135	130	95	6 6A 8 8A 18 18B 46 52 112 291
AD	Palmers Green	RT	73	55	46	29 34 102 112
AE	Hendon	STD, RT	92	93	63	13 83A 113 142 183
AF	Chelverton Road	RT	71	73	60	28 30 37
AH	Nunhead	RT, G	90	82	59	12 37 63 173
AK	Streatham	STL, RT	77	73	52	49 59A 118 133 159
AL	Merton	STL, D, Q	195	168	135	32 49 77 77A 88 93 118 127[3] 152 156 157 200
AM	Plumstead	RTL	93	78	57	53A 99 122 122A 153 161 186
AP	Seven Kings	STL, RTL	74	69	63	25A 26 86 86A 139 139A 145 147 148 150 298
AR	Tottenham	RTL, RTW, TD	156	141	109	34B 41 67 73 76 102 144 236 290
AV	Hounslow	STL, RT, LT	99	100	93	33 81 81A 98 98A 110 111 116 117 162 203 237
AW[4]	Abbey Wood	RTL	20	20	11	177 182
B	Battersea	STL, RTL, RTW	83	82	59	19 22 31 39 49 A[5]
BK	Barking	STL, RTL	140	129	96	9 23 23B 23C 62 62A 87 145 148 174 175 295
BN	Brixton	RT	92	79	47	50 57 95 109 133 287
C	Athol Street	STL, RTL	65	50	42	56 82 108 108A PLA[6]
CA	Clapham	RTL	130	121	79	45 50 104 137 155 168 169 181 189 189A 287
CF	Chalk Farm	STL, RTL, RTW, SRT	102	93	78	3 24 27A 27B 31 39 68 74 196
CL	Clay Hall	RTL, RTW	65	63	50	8 8A 10 25 56 60 PLA[6]
D	Dalston	RT, RTW, LT, Q	122	127	87	9 11 24 47 78 106 208 208A
E	Enfield	STD, G, RT, RTL, T, TD	114	103	88	102 107 107A 121 128 135 144A 144B 205 242 243
ED	Elmers End	RT	91	73	51	12 54 75 194
EW	Edgware	RT, TD	62	60	42	140 141 142 240A
F	Putney Bridge	RT, RTW	95	96	82	14 14A 74 85 93 96
G	Forest Gate	RT, SRT	113	98	81	25 66 96 145 147
GM	Victoria	STL, STD, RT	102	98	69	10 24 39 52 77 77A 134 137
H	Hackney	RT, RTL, RTW	97	82	70	6 6A 22 30 106
HD	Harrow Weald	ST, STL, RT, TD	85	87	64	114 140 158 209 221 230[3]
HW	Southall	STL, B, RT, TD	112	108	82	55 83 92 92A 97 105 120 120A 211
J	Holloway	RT	166	163	119	4 4A 14 14A 19 27 27A 27B 43 58 134 143 171 172 196 292
K	Kingston	STL, T, Q, TD	47	49	44	152 215 216 218 219
L	Loughton	STD, T	41	41	39	20 38A 167 254
M	Mortlake	RT	74	66	58	9 33 71 73
MH	Muswell Hill	RT, Q, TD	99	95	73	43 125 210 212 244 251 251A
N	Norwood	RT	74	65	48	2 3 68 195
NB[7]	Norbiton	RT, T	50	50	43	65 131 201 206 213 216 264 265
NX[8]	New Cross	STL, RT, RTL	79	85	48	21 163 177 182 186
ON	Alperton	STL, RT	81	72	53	18 79 83 83A 92 92A 187
P	Old Kent Road	RT, Q	93	88	56	4 17 21 53A 78 89 153 159 202 I-S[9]
PB	Potters Bar	RT	67	52	46	29 84 134 207
PM	Peckham	RT	119	92	75	12 36 36A 70 70A 78 173 188 286
Q	Camberwell	RTL, SRT	146	116	84	4A 35 35A 40 42 48 59A 77 137 196
R	Riverside	RTL, RTW	78	80	68	11 17 27 27A 27B 71 72 88 91 289 297
RD	Hornchurch	STL RTL, SRT, T, TD	98	98	77	66 86 86A 103 123 165 174 175 238 246 247 247A 248 249 250 252
RL[10]	Rye Lane	RT	99	63	63	1 12 69 149 172 179 285
S	Shepherd's Bush	RTL	43	34	36	12 105
SP	Sidcup	STL, RTL, Q, T	86	72	64	21 21A 51 51A 51B 132 161 228 229 241
SW[11]	Stockwell	STL, RTL	41	41	24	88 171 178 B[5]

Code	Garage	Types	M-F	Sat	Sun	Routes
T	Leyton	STD, RT, TD	156	138	114	10 35 35A 38 38A 106 144 236 296
TB	Bromley	RT, LT	91	91	71	47 61 94 119 126 138 146 227
TC	Croydon	RT, LT	146	138	108	12 59 64 115 130 133 159 166 166A 197 234 234A
TH	Thornton Heath	RT	54	40	31	59 109 190
TL	Catford	RT	188	179	139	1 47 54 75 89 94 124 160 180 186
U	Upton Park	STL, G, RT, RTW	203	180	130	15 23A 40 86 86A 100 101 129 145 175
UX	Uxbridge	STL, RT, T	53	55	43	98 98A 204 220 222 223 224 225
V	Turnham Green	RT	81	76	59	55 65 91 265
W	Cricklewood	STL, RT, SRT	158	147	117	1 2 13 16 60 112 142 226 240 294
WD	Wandsworth	RTL	72	69	43	28 44 91 168 [12] 170 288
WG	West Green	RTL, Q	78	78	59	29 144 144A 144B 233
WL	Walworth	RTL	97	78	54	36A 77A 176 176A 184 185
X	Middle Row	RT	84	82	63	7 7A 15 28 72 187
TOTALS			6064	5582	4309	

Class summary

Class summary	Number of buses scheduled		
	M-F	Sat	Sun
Double-deck			
ST	1	2	–
STL	358	239	127
STD	154	143	89
B	21	21	–
D	267	250	218
G	58	41	14
RT	3038	2837	2246
RTL	1158	1075	852
RTW	491	487	369
SRT	155	114	69
TOTAL DOUBLE-DECK	5701	5209	3984
Single-deck			
LT	71	72	52
T	87	102	91
Q	81	75	78
TD	124	124	104
TOTAL SINGLE-DECK	363	373	325
GRAND TOTAL	6064	5582	4309

BEA contract

Code	Garage	Coach type	Number of coaches scheduled		
			M-F	Sat	Sun
GM	Victoria (Gillingham St)	Commer	49	52	43
		4RF4	3	3	3
TOTALS			52	55	46

1 Patterns of routes operated by garages often varied between Monday-Friday and weekend schedules.

2 Routes 285-298 were Night Bus routes; all operated Sunday-Friday nights only except routes 294 and 298, which also operated Saturday nights.

3 Lowbridge route.

4 Former tram depot; bus allocation commenced 6 July 1952.

5 Festival Gardens route.

6 Port of London Authority route within London Docks (use restricted to Dock employees).

7 Opened 14 May 1952

8 Bus allocation from 6 July 1952. Due to a combination of ongoing building and works programme to convert NX from tram to motor-bus operation and a shortage of new vehicles, buses were housed at (and in some cases provided by) PM, Q and RL. Buses started to work out of NX from 22 October 1952.

9 Inter Station night route between main-line railway termini.

10 Opened 6 January 1952.

11 Opened 2 April 1952.

12 Night service also operated Sunday-Friday nights.

13 British European Airways contract for conveyance of airline passengers from Kensington Air Station to London (Heath Row) and Northolt airports. Eight vehicles also provided a night service, seven days a week.

Appendix 7

Country Bus & Coach Department bus garages — scheduled allocation (less duplicates) to routes at 2 January 1952 (immediately following full absorption of former Eastern National Grays-area routes)

Code	Garage	Bus types	Number of vehicles scheduled			Routes operated [1]
			M-F	Sat	Sun	
CM	Chelsham	RT, T, Q, C	40	41	34	403 403A 403B 408 453 464 465 470 485 706
CY	Crawley	STL, RT, Q, RF	17	18	13	405 424 426 434 438 438A 710
DG	Dunton Green	STL, RT, T, C	35	35	26	402 403 403A 403B 404 413 413A 421 431 431A 431B 431C 431D 454 454A 471 705
DS	Dorking	STL, RT, T, C, TF [2]	31	32	25	412 414 425 429 433 439 449 712 713 714
DT	Dartford	STL, RT	14	19	19	401 423 467 475 486 491
EG	East Grinstead	STL, RT, T, Q, C, CR	20	20	18	409 411 424 428 434 494 708
EP	Epping	RT, T, C, CR, TF	28	29	24	308 308A 339 381 384 384A 393 396 399 718 720
GD	Godstone	STL, RT, RLH, RF	37	38	30	409 410 [3] 411 709
GF	Guildford	STL, RT, T, Q, C	30	33	28	408 415 425 432 436 [3] 436A [3] 448 448A 463 [3] 470 715
GY	Grays	STL, RT, TF, T	73	53	45	323 323A 323B 328 328A 349 357 367 368 370 370A 371 371A 374 375 379 380 723 723A
HE	High Wycombe	STL, RT, T, RF	30	31	23	326 326A 362 362A 362B 363 366 455 455A 455B 711
HF	Hatfield	RT, T	26	25	18	303 303A 303B 330 340 341 717
HG	Hertford	STL, RT, T, Q, C	67	65	56	308 308A 310 310A 327 329 329A 330 331 333 333B 341 342 350 350A 372 384 384A 384B 386 386A 388 389 390 395 395A 399 715
HH	Hemel Hempstead	STL, RT, T, Q	43	37	32	301 301B 301C 302 307 307A 314 316 317 318B 319 320 322 337 352 377 377A 377B 378 708
HN	Hitchin	T, C	11	10	9	308 308A 364 383 384 384A 390 399 716
LH	Leatherhead	RT, T, Q	55	56	50	406 408 416 418 418A 419 422 435 462 468 470
LS	Luton	STL, RT, T, TF	22	22	17	321 356 360 364 376 376A 714
MA	Amersham	STL, RT, RLH, T, C, RF	49	45	35	305 305A 309 336 [3] 348 353 359 362 362A 362B 373 394 394A 394B 394C 397 398 398A 703 709 710
NF	Northfleet	STL, RT, T, Q, C	61	58	37	450 451 452 480 480A 487 487A 488 488A 489 489A 490 490A 492 495 495A 496 497 497A 701 702
RE	Romford	RT	31	25	22	721 722
RG	Reigate	STL, RT, Q, RF	49	51	40	405 406 406C 411 414 429 430 439 439A 440 440A 447 447A 447B 711
SA	St Albans	STL, RT, T, Q, TF	59	61	43	304 313 325 330 330A 338 341 343 354 355 358 365 369 382 391 391A 713
SJ	Swanley	STL, RT, T, C	26	24	20	401 401B 423 423A 423B 423D 477 478 479 703
ST	Staines	STL, RT, T	28	28	22	441 441D 443 460 466 466A 469 701 702
TG	Tring	RT, T, Q, C	16	15	14	301 352 387 707
TW	Tunbridge Wells	RF	8	8	7	704
WA	Watford (High St)	STL, RT	76	80	46	306 311 312 321 332 335 344 344A 344B 345 346 351
WR	Windsor	STL, RT, T, TF, RF	73	75	54	335 407 407A 417 441 441B 442 444 445 446 446A 446B 457 457A 457C 457D 458 459 484 484A 484B 484C 704 705 718
WT	Watford (Leavesden Road)	STL, RT, T, Q, C [4]	24	24	17	301A 309 318 318A 318B 318C 336A 361 385
WY	Addlestone	ST, STL, RLH, T	30	34	28	427 435 436 [3] 436A [3] 437 456 456B 461 [3] 461A [3] 462 462B 462C 463 [3] 716 717
TOTALS			1109	1092	852	

126

Number of buses scheduled			
Class summary	**M-F**	**Sat**	**Sun**
Double-deck			
ST/STL	153	134	93
RT	500	506	370
RLH	19	19	17
TOTAL DOUBLE-DECK	672	659	480
Single-deck			
T	198	199	170
Q	91	91	70
C/CR	47	44	33
TF	57	55	56
RF	44	44	43
TOTAL SINGLE-DECK	437	433	372
GRAND TOTAL	1109	1092	852

1 7xx-series numbers are Green Line routes
2 One TF class outstationed at Holmbury St Mary
3 Low-bridge bus route
4 One C class outstationed at Loudwater

Appendix 8
London Transport double-deck bus routes subject to low-bridge constraint, 1952

Route		Location of bridge(s)	Garage(s)	Number of vehicles scheduled			Vehicle class(es)	
				M-F	Sat	Sun	1 Jan	31 Dec
Central Area								
127	(Morden Stn–South Wimbledon Stn)	Cheam Common Road, Worcester Park	AL	9	6	–	D	RLH
230	(Rayners Lane Stn–Northwick Park Stn)	Headstone Drive and Christchurch Ave, Harrow	HD	13	14	8	ST, STL,	RLH
TOTALS:				22	20	8		
Country Area								
336	(Watford–Chesham)	White Lion Lane, Amersham Common	MA	5	5	3	RLH	RLH
410	(Bromley–Reigate)	Blue House Lane, Oxted	GD	13	13	13	STL, RLH	RLH
436 436A	(Staines–Guildford) (Staines–Ripley)	Chertsey Lane, Staines, and Guildford Road, Woking	GF/WY	6	6	6	STL, RLH	RLH
461	(Staines–Walton-on-Thames)	Chertsey Lane, Staines	WY¹	6	7	6	ST, STL, RLH	RLH
463	(Walton-on-Thames–Guildford)	Guildford Road, Woking	GF/WY	6	7	6	STL	RLH
TOTALS				36	38	34		

1 Includes allocation for route 461A (Ottershaw–Walton-on-Thames), which although not subject to height restriction was interworked with route 461 and thus operated with lowbridge buses.

Acknowledgements

A NUMBER of people have contributed in important ways towards the contents of this book, for which I am most grateful. That doyen of enthusiasts, John Gillham, who worked for London Transport in 1952, has given expert advice and guidance on a wide range of topics. Graham Page, who also embarked upon a successful career with London Transport, has given me detailed advice on all fare and ticket matters. He not only loaned the tickets illustrated but also contributed all the information on fares and tickets incorporated in Chapter 8. Other help in providing source material has come from R. J. Edgington, Gerald Mead, Lawrence Murphy,Derek Persson and David Ruddom. I am grateful to the staff of London's Transport Museum at Covent Garden Museum as well as John Hart, Honorary Librarian of The Omnibus Society's London Collection, for affording me access to archive material. Thanks too are due to the Archive Information Officer at the Meteorological Office, Bracknell, for providing information on 1952's weather. Mention of the PSV Circle in the Bibliography does not really do justice to the sheer volume of detailed information that can be gleaned from its publications, and I am most grateful for permission to extract appropriate details.

I am indebted to all the photographers who have loaned me considerable quantities of photographs for possible use in the book. In particular, special thanks are due to Nick Carter, Michael Dryhurst, John Gillham, Roy Marshall and Geoffrey Morant, who afforded me access to their entire collections of 1952 London Transport material. Kevin Lane, Tony Wright and Arnold Richardson were all kind enough to help me, at very short notice, with photographic services. Steve Donnelly and his staff at Aries Business Centre, Basingstoke, gave much willing support with manuscript preparation and presentation. Finally, I must extend thanks to my wife Rosalind for her support during the time devoted to writing this book.

Bibliography

Books

Dunbar, C. S., Price, J. H., and Wilson, B. G.:
London's Tramway Subway
(Light Railway Transport League, undated)

Gillham, J. C.:
London's Double-deck Buses, (Ian Allan, 1950)

Glazier, K.:
London Buses in the 1950s (Capital Transport, 1989)
RF (Capital Transport, 1991)
London Bus File 1950-1954 (Capital Transport, 1998)

Hambley, J. A. S.:
London Transport Buses and Coaches 1952
(Images/author, 1993)

Joyce, J.:
Operation Tramaway (Ian Allan, 1987)

Morris, O. J. *et al*:
Fares Please (Ian Allan, 1953)

Stewart, D.:
Electric to Diesel 1935-1962
(London Omnibus Traction Society, 1977)

Thompson, D.:
Special — London's Non-standard Trams and Track 1946-1952 (Sheaf Publishing, 1982)

Waller, M. H., and Waller, P.:
British and Irish Tramway Systems since 1945
(Ian Allan, 1992)

Weinreb, B., and Hibbert, C.:
The London Encyclopædia (MacMillan Reference Books, 1995)

Willoughby, D. W., and Oakley, E. R.:
London Transport Tramways Handbook (authors, 1972)

Journals, magazines etc (various issues)

Historical and current notes in connection with various tours (The Omnibus Society)

Fleet Histories, Supplements and News Sheets (PSV Circle)

Buses Illustrated (Ian Allan)

London Bus Magazine
(London Omnibus Traction Society)

Map

Harris, M.:
The 1952 Greater London Bus Map (compiler, 1999)